Secure TCP/IP Programming
with SSL

AuthorHouse™
1663 Liberty Drive, Suite 200
Bloomington, IN 47403
www.authorhouse.com
Phone: 1-800-839-8640

AuthorHouse™ UK Ltd.
500 Avebury Boulevard
Central Milton Keynes, MK9 2BE
www.authorhouse.co.uk
Phone: 08001974150

First published by AuthorHouse 3/7/07

ISBN: 978-1-4259-9221-7 (sc)
ISBN: 978-1-4259-9223-1 (dj)

Printed in the United States of America
Bloomington, Indiana

This book is printed on acid-free paper.

Secure TCP/IP Programming with SSL

Developer's Guide

Edward Zaremba

OpenSSL Documentation and Developer's Guide Disclaimer

This OpenSSL software is subject to U.S. Commerce Department export restrictions, and is intended for use in the country or countries into which Trizen released it. You agree to fully comply with all laws and regulations of the United States and other countries ("Export Laws") to assure that neither the Software nor any direct products thereof are (1) exported directly or indirectly in violation of Export Laws or (2) are used for any purpose prohibited by Export Laws including without limitation nuclear, chemical or biological weapons production. In particular but without limitation, none of the Software or underlying information or technology may be downloaded or otherwise exported or re-exported (i) into (or to a national or resident of) Cuba, Haiti, Iraq, Libya, Yugoslavia, North Korea, Iran, or Syria or (ii) to anyone on the US Treasury Department's list of Specially Designated Nationals or the US Commerce Department's Table of Deny Orders. By downloading the Software, you are agreeing to the foregoing and you are representing and warranting that you are not located in, under control of, or a national or resident of any such country or on any such list.

LIMITATION OF LIABILITY

TO THE MAXIMUM EXTENT PERMITTED BY APPLICABLE LAW, TRIZEN AND ITS SUPPLIERS DISCLAIM ALL OTHER WARRANTIES, EITHER EXPRESS OR IMPLIED, INCLUDING, BUT NOT LIMITED TO, ANY IMPLIED WARRANTIES OF MERCHANTABILITY, FITNESS FOR A PARTICULAR PURPOSE, NON-NFRINGEMENT OR TITLE, WITH REGARD TO THE SOFTWARE AND THE ACCOMPANYING DOCUMENTATION.

TO THE MAXIMUM EXTENT PERMITTED BY APPLICABLE LAW, IN NO EVENT SHALL TRIZEN OR ITS SUPPLIERS BE LIABLE FOR ANY DAMAGES WHATSOEVER (INCLUDING, WITHOUT LIMITATION, DAMAGES FOR LOSS OF BUSINESS PROFITS, BUSINESS INTERRUPTION, LOSS OF BUSINESS INFORMATION, OR ANY OTHER PECUNIARY LOSS) ARISING OUT OF THE USE OF OR INABILITY TO USE THIS OPENSSL PRODUCT EVEN IF TRIZEN HAS BEEN ADVISED OF THE POSSIBILITY OF SUCH DAMAGES. IN ANY CASE, TRIZEN'S ENTIRE LIABILITY UNDER ANY PROVISION OF THIS LICENSE AGREEMENT SHALL BE LIMITED TO US$0.

In general, the OpenSSL software, "software", is managed by the OpenSSL organization and is licensed under an Apache style license. If you use the software that is produced by the OpenSSL organization it is your responsibility to disclose and conform to any and all license requirements as dictated by the OpenSSL organization. THIS IS NOT A PRODUCT MANAGED OR DEVELOPED BY TRIZEN. TRIZEN IS PROVIDING

THIS MANUAL AS A SUPPLEMENT TO ANY DOCUMENTATION PROVIDED BY THE OPENSSL ORGANIZATION.

HIGH RISK ACTIVITIES

The Software is not fault-tolerant and is not designed, manufactured or intended for use or resale as on-line control equipment in hazardous environments requiring fail-safe performance, such as in the operation of nuclear facilities, aircraft navigation or communication systems, air traffic control, direct life support machines, or weapons systems, in which the failure of the Software could lead directly to death, personal injury, or severe physical or environmental damage ("High Risk Activities"). Trizen and its suppliers specifically disclaim any express or implied warranty of fitness for High Risk Activities.

OPENSSL DISCLAIMER

This software package uses strong cryptography, so even if it is created, maintained and distributed from liberal countries in Europe (where it is legal to do this), it falls under certain export/import and/or use restrictions in some other parts of the world.

PLEASE REMEMBER THAT EXPORT/IMPORT AND/OR USE OF STRONG CRYPTOGRAPHY SOFTWARE, PROVIDING CRYPTOGRAPHY HOOKS OR EVEN JUST COMMUNICATING TECHNICAL DETAILS ABOUT CRYPTOGRAPHY SOFTWARE IS ILLEGAL IN SOME PARTS OF THE WORLD. SO, WHEN YOU IMPORT THIS PACKAGE TO YOUR COUNTRY, RE-DISTRIBUTE IT FROM THERE OR EVEN JUST EMAIL TECHNICAL SUGGESTIONS OR EVEN SOURCE PATCHES TO THE AUTHOR OR OTHER PEOPLE YOU ARE STRONGLY ADVISED TO PAY CLOSE ATTENTION TO ANY EXPORT/IMPORT AND/OR USE LAWS WHICH APPLY TO YOU. THE AUTHORS OF OPENSSL ARE NOT LIABLE FOR ANY VIOLATIONS YOU MAKE HERE. SO BE CAREFUL, IT IS YOUR RESPONSIBILITY.

CREDIT INFORMATION: This product includes cryptographic software written by Eric A. Young (eay@cryptsoft.com). This product includes software written by Tim J. Hudson (tjh@cryptsoft.com).

Acknowledgements

I would like to thank my wife Anna, my son Caden and my daughter Karissa. I would also like to thank my mother Charlene Hogan and my father Edward Zaremba for giving me my first computer back in 1983, a Texas instrumens TI/99-4A which unleashed my passion for computing and my first foray into programming—"Frogger for the TI." I would also like to thank my other family members, Jeff Hogan, Judd Hogan, Sarah Hogan and of course my grandmother Juanita and my grandfather Ted.

A very special thank you goes to Nicolette Corso-Vilmos for making me write this book. Thanks also goes to my wife's family Stan and Stasia Wilzak and their children Tomek and Marcin Wilczak as well as the AuthorHOUSE family, my publishers, for their support in completing this small but special book for me.

And last but not least I would like to thank my professors from Florida State University, the University of Southern Mississippi and Tallahassee Community College: Dr. Fay, Dr. Redfurn, Dr. Jones, Dr. Hinson, and many many more who influenced my studies including Dr. Foss and Dr. Abele from FSU.

This book is dedicated to all those brave souls who venture into the world of encryption and secure communication.

Contents

Introducing OpenSSL

"The OpenSSL Project is a collaborative effort to develop a robust, commercial-grade, full-featured, and Open Source toolkit implementing the Secure Sockets Layer (SSL v2/v3) and Transport Layer Security (TLS v1) protocols as well as a full-strength general purpose cryptography library. The project is managed by a worldwide community of volunteers that use the Internet to communicate, plan, and develop the OpenSSL toolkit and its related documentation."

-OpenSSL Organization

Before you Begin

This guide makes several assumptions: 1) You have a Visual C++ compiler version 6.0 or higher. 2) You are an experienced programmer using C++. 3) You have familiarity with the MS-DOS operating system and command line utilities.

The manual is intended for developers interested in using the OpenSSL toolkit and interested in using the OpenSSL libraries within their applications. It is also useful for gaining insight into Public Key Infrastructure (PKI) and Certificate Authority management as well as the usefulness of the OpenSSL command line tools.

What's Included in the Developer's Guide?

The OpenSSL for Windows Developer's Guide is made up of the following chapters:

Building the OpenSSL Libraries	This chapter focuses on Downloading and Building OpenSSL
Creating a Certificate Authority	Describes Creating, Issuing, and Signing Certificates within Windows
Using s_server & s_client	Describes using the two most important utilities in OpenSSL
OpenSSL Utilities	Using other OpenSSL Utilities
Authenticode	Digitally Sign your applications, use an SSL

Server Certificate

Building the OpenSSL Libraries

In order to use the OpenSSL toolkit you must download it from the OpenSSL web site. This is fairly straightforward. If you simply need the binaries, you may simply download them from www.openssl.org and make use of them pre-built.

1) Visit http://www.openssl.org/source and download the latest (non-engine) tarball. A tarball, UNIX related, is similar to a zip file. Save the file anywhere on your hard drive, but remember its location.

2) Download and/or purchase WinZip at http://www.winzip.com. We recommend you spend the $40 to purchase a licensed copy of WinZip.

3) Go to the location where you downloaded and saved the openssl zip/tar file. If you are using WinZip as your registered zip utility, it should have a WinZip icon. Just double click on the icon.

openssl-0.9.6a
.tar.gz

3.1) If you see the following dialog, just press Yes to Continue:

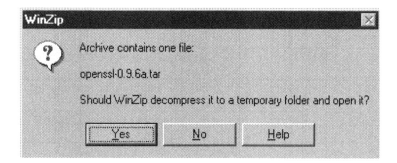

3.2) You should see the following dialog. Notice that this is a very large file. Also note that there are almost 1500 files associated with the tarball.

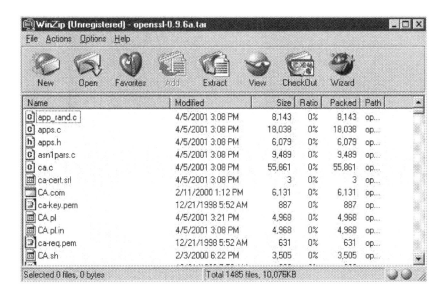

4) Extract the files to C:\OpenSSL by selecting Actions | Extract. Create the OpenSSL directory in the "Extract to:" field by making your screen look similar to the next image then click Extract.

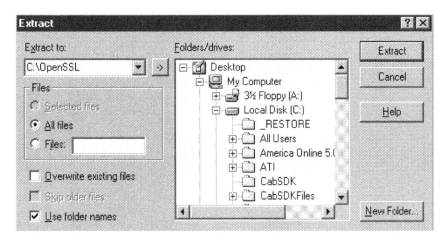

4.1)   This new OpenSSL directory will now house a new folder titled:

openssl-0.9.6a

4.2)   The latest version may have a **different version** number than the
        above, but it should be similar. You can close the WinZip
        application. But notice that there is no MSVC folder within the
        openssl-9.6.a folder. This will be installed later.

5) Download the MS Developer Studio Workspace by visiting
    http://www.openssl.org and locate the MS Dev Studio workspace for
    OpenSSL like and follow the directions to download the version
    without masm or nasm. If you cannot locate the file, a version is
    located at http://www.trizen.com/openssl. This file should be
    VC6ossl096a.zip noting that version numbers may differ slightly.
    Assembler versions will have a 'masm' or 'nasm' included in the
    title—DO NOT DOWNLOAD these. Save this zip file anywhere on
    your hard drive by clicking on its link or Shift+click on its link, but
    remember its location. If the above website is unavailable then visit
    the OpenSSL website and look for related information, which should
    have a link.

6) Double click on the saved VC6ossl096a.zip file (the version number
    may be different) which will open up the WinZip utility. You must
    extract this file into the above **openssl-0.9.6a** directory created earlier
    in step 4.

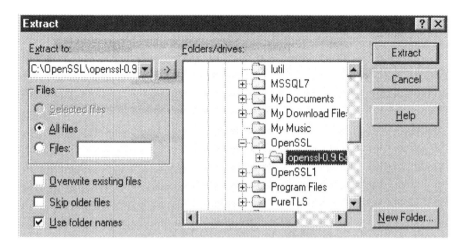

6.1)   NOTE: Upon extracting the file into this directory you should
        have the following directory structure (with the new MSVC
        directory):

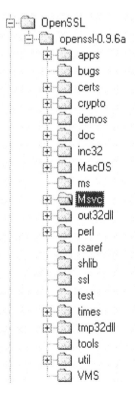

7) If you have not already done so, you must install Visual C++ 6.0. Remembering to run the VCVARS32.bat file. This file is located in the VC98 directory of the Microsoft Visual Studio folder. Just double click on the VCVARS32.bat file.

8) You must now download Perl for Windows. We have chosen ActivePerl and it can be downloaded at http://www.activestate.com/Products/ActivePerl/. Of course any Perl for Windows will work, but make sure that your PATH variable has the location of the Perl.exe file appended to the PATH variable string after you have installed ActivePerl. This can be checked in Windows ME by going to Start | Run and typing MSCONFIG.EXE. You should see the following dialog, noting that the installation location for this example is *c:\Perl\bin*. This is the directory path to where the Perl.exe file was installed. By adding this location to your path variable you can issue a Perl command from any DOS prompt without having to be in the same directory as the Perl.exe file.

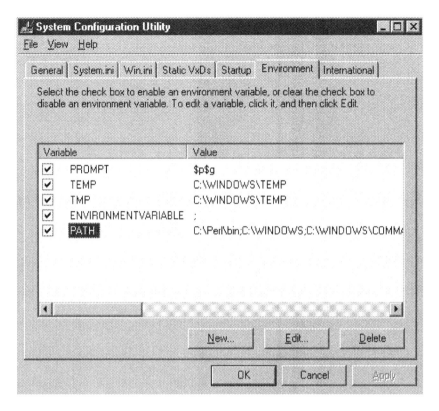

9) Notice the new C:\Perl\bin entry in the PATH variable. Again, this location represents this example. The location where you install Perl may differ slightly. Just make sure that the directory to the Perl.exe file that is installed with ActivePerl is appended somewhere in the PATH variable string. Windows NT users can access the PATH variable by right clicking on the *My Computer* icon, selecting the Advanced tab and then clicking on the Environment Variables button. For other operating systems, please see your Windows OS documentation for PATH variables.

10) Once you have a Perl program installed, you should copy the command.com (cmd.exe for NT) to the openssl-0.9.6a directory. This will allow you to run the necessary Perl scripts provided with the OpenSSL toolkit. The command.com or cmd.exe file can be found in your Windows or WINNT directory. Users of Windows NT/2000/XP must use cmd.exe.

11) Double click on the new command.com file (or cmd.exe) in your openssl-0.9.6a directory. At the command prompt type the following and press enter noting that this command is <u>case sensitive</u>:

C:\OpenSSL\openssl-0.9.6a>*Perl Configure VC-WIN32*

You should see something similar to the following screen:

```
MS-DOS Prompt
T  8 x 13

c:\OpenSSL1\openssl-0.9.6a>perl configure VC-WIN32
Configuring for VC-WIN32
Iswindows=1
CC                =cl
CFLAG             =-DTHREADS  -DDSO_WIN32
EX_LIBS           =
BN_ASM            =bn_asm.o
DES_ENC           =des_enc.o fcrypt_b.o
BF_ENC            =bf_enc.o
CAST_ENC          =c_enc.o
RC4_ENC           =rc4_enc.o
RC5_ENC           =rc5_enc.o
MD5_OBJ_ASM       =
SHA1_OBJ_ASM      =
RMD160_OBJ_ASM=
PROCESSOR         =
RANLIB            =true
PERL              =perl
THIRTY_TWO_BIT mode
BN_LLONG mode
RC4_INDEX mode
RC4_CHUNK is undefined

Configured for VC-WIN32.

c:\OpenSSL1\openssl-0.9.6a>_
```

11.1) If you don't see the above information after you type the *Perl Configure VC-WIN32* command you should review your steps and possibly delete the OpenSSL directory, extracting the files again and starting over. If you get an error that states:

"'perl is not recognized as an internal or external operable program or batch file"

11.2)   If you get the above message, then check to make sure you have installed Perl and that the directory location of Perl.exe is contained somewhere in the PATH system variable.

12)   At the same command prompt type the following and press enter:

C:\OpenSSL\openssl1-0.9.6a>ms*do_ms.bat*

You should see something similar to the following screen:

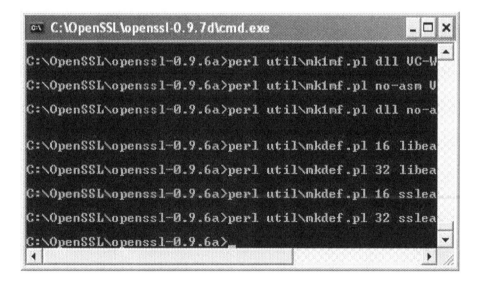

12.1)   If you don't see something similar to the above, you may have to start over making sure you have typed everything correctly and placed the extracted files in the right directories.

13)   At the same command prompt type the following and press enter. The directory may be msvc\ or msvc097\, just make sure you are targeting the msvc* directory :

C:\OpenSSL\openssl-0.9.6a>*perl msvc\doinc.pl*

13.1) If all goes well, the screen should pause for a second and then basically return the command prompt. This command will create three (3) new directories in the openssl-0.9.6a directory:

- inc32
- out32dll
- tmp32dll

13.2) The most important of these is the out32dll directory which will have the Microsoft Visual C++ Release and Debug directories. Within these directories will be the OpenSSL libraries after a successful build in Visual C++. At this point you should check the openssl-0.9.6a directory to make sure these were successfully created.

13.3) If these directories do not appear in your openssl-0.9.6a then try starting from the beginning making sure you follow each step carefully.

14) Open Visual C++ and open the OpenSSL.dsw file in the newly created msvc directory within the openssl-0.9.6a directory. You may have to select *.dsw from the types of files to view in the Open project dialog.

15) You should see approximately 59 or so projects. The most important projects being the SSLeay32 and Libeay32 projects. Other important projects are the s_server and s_client projects.

16) At this point you should perform a batch build by selecting from the menu bar, Build | Batch Build. Press the *Rebuild All* button on the resulting form making sure that all projects are checked:

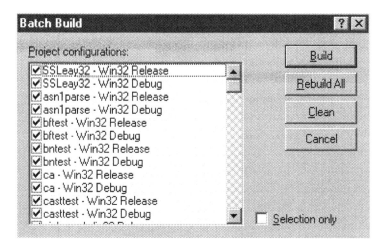

16.1) This will take upwards of 10 minutes to compile all the projects including the Debug and Release versions. You should hear several windows attention "beeps" as the compiler moves from project to project.

17) At this point the OpenSSL libraries: SSLeay32.dll and Libeay32.dll can be utilized in your applications. They can be found in the Release directory of the out32dll directory within the openssl-0.9.6a directory.

18) **APPEND YOUR PATH VARIABLE TO POINT TO THE NEW RELEASE DIRECTORY UNDER THE OUT32DLL i.e. PATH=c:\OpenSSL\openssl-0.9.6a\out32dll\release. Make sure that the OpenSSL release directory for the correct version is contained in the PATH variable or you will not be able to execute the OpenSSL commands from anywhere but the release directory.**

Creating Your Own Certificate Authority

What is a Certificate Authority? A Certificate Authority is a clearinghouse of sorts that will provide a signed certificate that you may use in your applications. Some of the most notable are Verisign and Thawte which provide SSL certificates for use within web servers as well as Authenticode certificates for Microsoft ActiveX distribution. These certificates enable encryption as well as provide a "security blanket" of sorts that ensures a company is safe to communicate with.

By creating your own certificate authority, developers can utilize their own certificates in their applications. Visual 3270 and Visual SSL, products designed by Trizen all use certificates created by a Certificate Authority under a Trizen server. If you want to create your own certificates then you must create a CA structure on your network that can be accessed.

Of course you can get started right away by using the *server.pem* and/or *client.pem* files that come with OpenSSL. These files can be found in *c:\OpenSSL\openssl-0.9.6a\apps* directory.

Creating the Directory Structure

This is relatively painless. Create a directory named CARoot anywhere on your hard drive. For this documentation we are creating a new directory at c:\CARoot. Within this directory create four new directories so that your directory structure looks similar to the following:

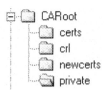

Creating the Random File (.rnd)

First, copy the command.com or cmd.exe file to the *CARoot* directory. Next, create a .rnd file in the new private subdirectory—the tricky part is saving it without a prefix so that it is named ".rnd" rather than "random.rnd" or something similar. To do this in windows, double click on the command.com or cmd.exe file in the *CARoot* directory. At the MS-DOS (command) prompt type the following and press enter to create the ".rnd" file without a prefix:

>   C:\CARoot>*edit private\.rnd*

When the MS-DOS text edit fills the screen, just type in a bunch of data or open up a file of data such as an executable file, then save the file. You should now have a ".rnd" file located in the *CARoot\private* directory. If you don't have a ".rnd" file, then make sure you follow the directions exactly as outlined.

Creating the CA Key File

At this point you must make your Certificate Authority(CA) private key and certificate files. These files will be utilized when creating other certificates signed by your own Certificate Authority. You will be using the command prompt many times, so to save on navigation you should have already placed another copy of the command.com or cmd.exe file into:

>   *c:\CARoot*

Double click on this file (command.com or cmd.com) unless its already open, and from the command prompt type the following and then press enter:

>   C:\CARoot>*genrsa –out private\ca.key –rand private\.rnd 2048*

NOTE: Switches and Options that are usually preceded by a '—' are used to specify certain attributes or properties of the command. There should be a space before the '—' and after the switch/option

---

The above command will generate an RSA Key file that will represent the CA Key file and will be used to generate public certificates. Double check to make sure the *ca.key* file is now in the *private* directory in the *CARoot* directory that was created earlier. If you get an error saying "bad command" then make sure you have modified your PATH environment variable to point to *c:\OpenSSL\openssl-0.9.6a\out32dll\release* directory (see Building the OpenSSL Libraries). If all has gone well then you should have seen something similar to the following screen shot:

```
C:\OpenSSL\openssl-0.9.6a\cmd.exe                    _ □ ✕

C:\CARoot>genrsa -out private\ca.key -rand private\.rn
Loading 'screen' into random state - done
151 semi-random bytes loaded
Generating RSA private key, 2048 bit long modulus
.....................................................
..............+++
e is 65537 (0x10001)

C:\CARoot>_
```

If you want to add a password to your private key file, which is highly recommended, then perform the following command writing over the existing file:

C:\CARoot>*genrsa –out private\ca.key –rand private\.rnd –des3 2048*

Notice that all we added was the *–des3* switch. If you would like to see more information about this command type:

C:\CARoot*genrsa –help*

You may use this switch for any of the OpenSSL commands and comes in quite handy when you forget a switch option.

Creating the Config File (OpenSSL.cnf)

The Config file, named *OpenSSL.cnf,* is used for creating public certificates. The config file has all the information necessary to reproduce a public certificate based on the CA architecture and the CA Key file. A sample of a config file is provided in the OpenSSL apps directory. Unfortunately, Windows views any file with a .cnf extension as a *speed dial* file and may be tough to locate; however, look for a file named "openssl" without a visible extension with a "speed dial" association:

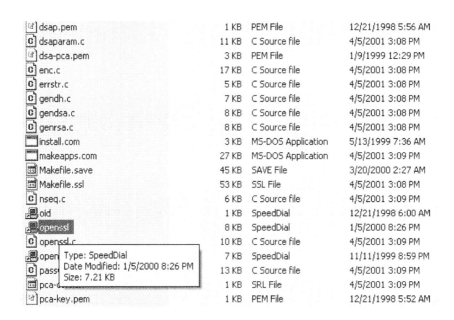

Copy this file from the OpenSSL apps directory to the CARoot directory. If not already open, double click on the command.com or cmd.exe file in the CARoot directory and type the following into the MS-DOS prompt:

C:\CARoot>edit openssl.cnf

This will bring up the MS-DOS editor with the openssl.cnf file opened for editing. The following snippet represents Trizen's configuration file:

```
# OpenSSL example configuration file.
```

```
# This is mostly being used for generation of certificate
requests.
#

# This definition stops the following lines choking if HOME
isn't
# defined.
HOME            = .
RANDFILE        = $ENV::HOME/.rnd

# Extra OBJECT IDENTIFIER info:
#oid_file       = $ENV::HOME/.oid
oid_section     = new_oids

# To use this configuration file with the "-extfile" option of
the
# "openssl x509" utility, name here the section containing the
# X.509v3 extensions to use:
# extensions    =
# (Alternatively, use a configuration file that has only
# X.509v3 extensions in its main [= default] section.)

[ new_oids ]

# We can add new OIDs in here for use by 'ca' and 'req'.
# Add a simple OID like this:
# testoid1=1.2.3.4
# Or use config file substitution like this:
# testoid2=${testoid1}.5.6

################################################################
#####
[ ca ]
default_ca      = CA_default        # The default ca section

################################################################
#####
[ CA_default ]

dir             = .                 # Where everything is kept
certs           = $dir/certs        # Where the issued certs are kept
crl_dir         = $dir/crl          # Where the issued crl are kept
database        = $dir/index.txt    # database index file.
new_certs_dir   = $dir/newcerts     # default place for new certs.
certificate     = $dir/private/ca.crt  # The CA certificate
serial          = $dir/serial       # The current serial number
crl             = $dir/crl.pem      # The current CRL
private_key     = $dir/private/ca.key # The private key
RANDFILE        = $dir/private/.rnd   # random data to use with certs
```

The most important components are the highlighted items and are discussed as follows:

1. dir: Should be "." which means "the current directory where this (openssl.cnf) configuration file is located."
2. certs: where issued or requested certificates should be saved.
3. crl_dir: Certificate Revocation Lists, those certificates that are should no longer be accepted.
4. database: a text (index.txt) file that will hold the increment of the certificates issued.
5. new_certs_dir: Signed certificates will be placed here (C:\CARoot\newcerts).
6. certificate: The CA Certificate derived from the CA Key (ca.crt).
7. serial: Each certificate is given a serial number as it is created, this keeps the increment.
8. private_key: The CA Key file. Keep this private (ca.key).
9. RANDFILE: The file that will be used in creating keys. It should be noted that some attacks and breaches of encryption have been accomplished by using the random number. Keep this private.

Other elements are used in developing public certificates, such as what questions will be asked, how they will be asked and other defaults. You may notice later in the configuration file that the default country may be AU, you should change this to reflect your country such as US. At this point make all the modification highlighted above to the openssl.cnf file in the MS-DOS editor.

After you have made the sample configuration file (openssl.cnf) match the above, save it in the c:\CARoot directory. You will now have an openssl.cnf file in the CARoot folder (directory).

Having problems opening the Configuration File

If you're having problems opening the file in Windows, don't be alarmed. From an MS-DOS prompt, navigate to the openssl.cnf file. At the prompt type the following and press enter:

C:\OpenSSL\openssl-0.9.6a\apps>*edit openssl.cnf*

This will bring up the file in an MS-DOS editor. You can now make your changes and then save the file to the CARoot directory.

Creating the Database (index.txt) and Serial files for the CA

You should take note of the database entry in the openssl.cnf Configuration file above which points to a file named *index.txt*. This file is made up of line entries for each new certificate signed by the CA. To create the index file, type the following at the C:\CARoot file then press enter:

C:\CARoot>*touch .\index.txt*

NOTE: Touch is a program that will set the file's timestamp to the current system time. If you don't have the touch.exe file or equivalent, don't worry, just create a text file named *index.txt* in the *CARoot* directory.

You must now create the serial file. This file can be created by typing the following at the MS-DOS prompt and then press enter:

C:\CARoot>*echo 01 > serial*

This will create a file named *serial* in the *CARoot* directory. You can open this file with WordPad or Notepad (right click on the file, select "Open with" and then select "WordPad"). If you open the file you will see it contains one line with the text "01" without the quotes. OpenSSL documentation uses double quotes around the '01'; however, this will not work in Windows. Ensure no quotes exist around the 01.

To summarize, you should now have two files in the *CARoot* directory named *serial* and *index.txt*. Note that these two files are documented in the Configuration file (openssl.cnf) with the names: database (for the index.txt) and serial (for the serial file). Make sure that these files are in the C:\CARoot directory and not any sub directories.

Creating the CA Certificate

At this point you can now successfully create the CA Certificate. Make sure you have updated the PATH environment variable to reflect the *[c]:\OpenSSL\openssl-0.9.6a\out32dll\release* files that have been created in the OpenSSL Visual C++ build (your path may differ slightly from the above). Double click on the command.com or cmd.exe file located in your *CARoot* directory. At the command prompt type the following and press enter:

> C:\CARoot>*req –new –x509 –days 3650 –key private\ca.key –out private\ca.crt –config openssl.cnf*

```
C:\OpenSSL\openssl-0.9.6a\cmd.exe                    _ □ X
There are quite a few fields but you can leave some bl
For some fields there will be a default value,
If you enter '.', the field will be left blank.

Country Name (2 letter code) [US]:
State or Province Name (full name) [Some-State]:Florid
Locality Name (eg, city) []:Sanford
Organization Name (eg, company) [Internet Widgits Pty
Organizational Unit Name (eg, section) []:IT
Common Name (eg, YOUR name) []:
Email Address []:zaremba@trizen.com
```

Notice in the above screen shot that we were asked a series of questions. As you create your certificates you should use your own CA information being aware that you should give your certificate a long expiration date such as the 10 year date above. Notice also the question text is derived from the configuration file (openssl.cnf). Also notice that nothing has been added to any other directory such as the *newcerts* directory after this command. Remember, when using the req.exe application above, you are creating a self signed certificate! A self signed certificate is "dummy" certificate and has not been signed by a Certificate Authority. If you have turned on any client or server verification, it will fail with a return code of (18), which means a self signed certificate. For CA Certificates, they are all self-signed because you are the top of the chain; however, when you create other certificates, you will sign those certificates with your CA information! The following represents what your self signed CA certificate should now look like if opened in WordPad:

```
-----BEGIN CERTIFICATE-----
MIIEhTCCA22gAwIBAgIBADANBgkqhkiG9w0BAQQFADCBjTELMAkGA1UEBhMCVVMx
CzAJBgNVBAgTAkZMMREwDwYDVQQHEwhIZWF0aHJvdzEPMA0GA1UEChMGVHJpemVu
MREwDwYDVQQLEwhTb2Z0d2FyZTEXMBUGA1UEAxMOd3d3LnRyaXplbi5jb20xITAf
BgkqhkiG9w0BCQEWEnphcmVtYmFdHJpemVuLmNvbTAeFw0wMTEwMjAwMDAwNTZa
Fw0wMjEwMjAwMDAwNTZaMIGNMQswCQYDVQQGEwJVUzELMAkGA1UECBMCRkwxETAP
BgNVBAcTCEhlYXRocm93MQ8wDQYDVQQKEwZUcml6ZW4xETAPBgNVBAsTCFNvZnR3
YXJlMRcwFQYDVQQDEw53d3cudHJpemVuLmNvbTEhMB8GCSqGSIb3DQEJARYSemFy
ZW1iYUB0cml6ZW4uY29tMIIBIjANBgkqhkiG9w0BAQEFAAOCAQ8AMIIBCgKCAQEA
yldagYx3PusRilolOskdNX9YtnYAw+GL/uL+VyZb6qIqDQdiUnzZIHEQKCtMGcwN
Gc6IFU78aDfR8Hxf5D5mwe3uzlBh9zO4N9dZgKvW6B9eDuvY8EVuLuFq3JvZS5Wj
v9W3IwVf//2wauDyF/i/Vs+C8DcJLvV/iDLXgJVmAMJknum/nLBiz2rmNvdiANyB
gQJpiyAmESYAVcOpOhr5uuHDfxlmERpP14Ca3Vyhryp+se/T92sbhahupMBGufd4
fJ0OO0JvuSuP4Wim6GETW4bUCvDIJuTvoN9Mq6Gq7IVmtEzJDCRY32xWguz/U26/
5UIzNGGeExwA6VWC8edDbQIDAQABo4HtMIHqMB0GA1UdDgQWBBQkmWA4HTAJeAO4
N3K9lIBpf8FUVTCBugYDVR0jBIGyMIGvgBQkmWA4HTAJeAO4N3K9lIBpf8FUVaGB
k6SBkDCBjTELMAkGA1UEBhMCVVMxCzAJBgNVBAgTAkZMMREwDwYDVQQHEwhIZWF0
aHJvdzEPMA0GA1UEChMGVHJpemVuMREwDwYDVQQLEwhTb2Z0d2FyZTEXMBUGA1UE
AxMOd3d3LnRyaXplbi5jb20xITAfBgkqhkiG9w0BCQEWEnphcmVtYmFdHJpemVu
LmNvbYIBADAMBgNVHRMEBTADAQH/MA0GCSqGSIb3DQEBBAUAA4IBAQCcn/7S9wQZ
/YytEEAnIXShIvwIRKeJF1Qj7IBN1nLRQclctZFs3tveLYPt2xr+AXcrgIq07JPN
ev33qpCxrBBDcpV5OSYHftZV7Ah3dbjR2Jb95nMWBIXONcZkeMbGjQjY7wMLnHvB
8E3vwTWdmVSFfFs7JT2BNhphuT5kuhqo6NEaHNtA9vKZGPBGJrgLF8PoXCk0J8vR
L5WP8z5Kqelo4/9BT1WD0re6NtUh36XB1rNZfVuR01HshMNah5VL6UXRi5/pdttZ
uKdwIWpSs1YPIhR4MxFkHm4xif++pdN69ld6RHOpFs/1IS5rCEwBYrEPoSxjV7ud
QCAx3UW8vk6x
-----END CERTIFICATE-----
```

This is very standard stuff for self signed certificates, very simple with all the information encoded between the BEGIN CERTIFICATE and the END CERTIFICATE. At this point you have successfully created your CA Public Certificate and your CA Private Key files which should be kept in the *c:\CARoot\private directory*.

Creating a NEW Public Certificate and Key Pair

At this point you have a very basic CA structure but you can create certificates and sign them with your organization. We are going to walk you through creating a key pair:

1) Create a new Key file using the genrsa.exe command:

   C:\CARoot>*genrsa –out cert.key –rand private\.rnd 2048*

2) Or Create a new Key file with a password using the genrsa command:

   C:\CARoot>*genrsa –out cert.key –rand private\.rnd –des3 2048*

If all goes well your should see something similar to the previous screen shot. It is HIGHLY recommended that you use passwords to encrypt your key files for servers; however, there is no reason for client files to be encrypted with a password. If you forget your password you will have to recreate your certificate.

3) Create a Public Certificate using the req.exe command as detailed in the screen shot:

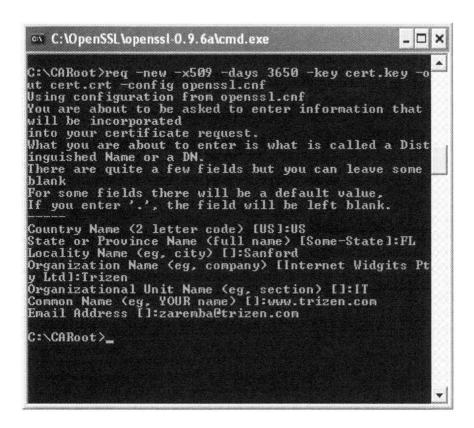

If all goes well you should see the above screen shot. Note the questions that were asked and how they match with the openssl.cnf file modified earlier. You may at anytime open this configuration file and change the defaults. At this point you should have a cert.key and a cert.crt file in your CARoot directory. If these files do not exist, double check your work and try again. You should note that the new cert.crt file has not been signed and is very similar to the CA certificate at this point. The next step is to sign the certificate with your CA key file.

4) Sign the certificate using the following command:

C:\CARoot>*ca –ss_cert cert.crt –key private\ca.key –config openssl.cnf –policy policy_anything –out signedcert.crt*

Note: Do not use the *cert.key* as this is the newly generated Key (use it for generating a public key, not signing the key), you must use the CA Key file generated earlier to establish the certificate chain.

In the above if we did not use the *–policy policy_anything* switch to accept the certificate as it currently exists the ca.exe command would complain. Once you have signed the certificate, one will be located in your *newcerts* directory as a record of the transaction with the serial number and a .pem extension i.e. *01.pem*. For each newly signed certificate, your newcerts directory will be updated, increasing the index number for each new certificate. The other location is in the CARoot directory and is the signedcert.crt file as specified in the *–out* parameter. Use this file, along with the cert.key file, in your OpenSSL applications. IF YOU HAVE ANY PROBLEMS make sure your openssl.cnf file was created correctly!

Note: You may delete certificates the *index.txt* file if you want to recreate or resign the certificates. You may also change the sequence number in the *serial* file.

You should see a lot of information fly by when you issue the above command and then you should be asked if you want to sign the certificate? Just press Y and then press enter. You will then be asked if you want to "commit" the file. Just press Y and then press enter. You should see more information fly by and finally end with "database updated."

```
C:\OpenSSL\openssl-0.9.6a\cmd.exe                    _ □ X

C:\CARoot>ca -ss_cert cert.crt -key private\ca.key -con
olicy_anything -out signedcert.crt
Using configuration from openssl.cnf
Loading 'screen' into random state - done
Check that the request matches the signature
Signature ok
The Subjects Distinguished Name is as follows
countryName               :PRINTABLE:'US'
stateOrProvinceName       :PRINTABLE:'FL'
localityName              :PRINTABLE:'Sanford'
organizationName          :PRINTABLE:'Trizen'
organizationalUnitName    :PRINTABLE:'IT'
commonName                :PRINTABLE:'www.trizen.com'
emailAddress              :IA5STRING:'zaremba@trizen.com'
Certificate is to be certified until Dec 28 16:05:05 20
Sign the certificate? [y/n]:y


1 out of 1 certificate requests certified, commit? [y/n
Write out database with 1 new entries
Data Base Updated

C:\CARoot>
```

The above screen shot represents the typical "signing" process. If you did not see something similar to the above, then repeat the steps making sure you followed the examples explicitly.

If you check the *newcerts* directory you should see a new certificate in the directory with a *01.pem* filename (may be a different number, but it will be the highest). If you look at the file you should see something similar to the following:

```
Data:
        Version: 3 (0x2)
        Serial Number: 1 (0x1)
        Signature Algorithm: md5WithRSAEncryption
        Issuer: C=US, ST=FL, L=Heathrow, O=Trizen, OU=Software,
CN=www.trizen.com/Email=zaremba@trizen.com
        Validity
            Not Before: Oct 20 00:02:05 2001 GMT
            Not After : Oct 20 00:02:05 2002 GMT
        Subject: C=US, ST=FL, O=Trizen, OU=Software,
CN=www.trizen.com/Email=zaremba@trizen.com
        Subject Public Key Info:
            Public Key Algorithm: rsaEncryption
            RSA Public Key: (2048 bit)
```

```
            Modulus (2048 bit):
                00:ca:57:5a:81:8c:77:3e:eb:11:8b:5a:25:3a:c9:
                1d:35:7f:58:b6:76:00:c3:e1:8b:fe:e2:fe:57:26:
                5b:ea:a2:2a:0d:07:62:52:7c:d9:20:71:10:28:2b:
                4c:19:cc:0d:19:ce:88:15:4e:fc:68:37:d1:f0:7c:
                5f:e4:3e:66:c1:ed:ee:ce:50:61:f7:33:b8:37:d7:
                59:80:ab:d6:e8:1f:5e:0e:eb:d8:f0:45:6e:2e:e1:
                6a:dc:9b:d9:4b:95:a3:bf:d5:b7:23:05:5f:ff:fd:
                b0:6a:e0:f2:17:f8:bf:56:cf:82:f0:37:09:2e:f5:
                7f:88:32:d7:80:95:66:00:c2:64:9e:e9:bf:9c:b0:
                62:cf:6a:e6:36:f7:62:00:dc:81:81:02:69:8b:20:
                26:11:26:00:55:c3:a9:3a:1a:f9:ba:e1:c3:7f:19:
                66:11:1a:4f:d7:80:9a:dd:5c:a1:af:2a:7e:b1:ef:
                d3:f7:6b:1b:85:a8:6e:a4:c0:46:b9:f7:78:7c:9d:
                34:3b:42:6f:b9:2b:8f:e1:68:a6:e8:61:13:5b:86:
                d4:0a:f0:c8:26:e4:ef:a0:df:4c:ab:a1:aa:ec:85:
                66:b4:4c:c9:0c:24:58:df:6c:56:82:ec:ff:53:6e:
                bf:e5:42:33:34:61:9e:13:1c:00:e9:55:82:f1:e7:
                43:6d
            Exponent: 65537 (0x10001)
        X509v3 extensions:
            X509v3 Basic Constraints:
                CA:FALSE
            Netscape Comment:
                OpenSSL Generated Certificate
            X509v3 Subject Key Identifier:

24:99:60:38:1D:30:09:78:03:B8:37:72:BD:94:80:69:7F:C1:54:55
            X509v3 Authority Key Identifier:

keyid:24:99:60:38:1D:30:09:78:03:B8:37:72:BD:94:80:69:7F:C1:54:55

DirName:/C=US/ST=FL/L=Heathrow/O=Trizen/OU=Software/CN=www.trizen.com/Email=zaremba@trizen.com
                serial:00

    Signature Algorithm: md5WithRSAEncryption
        7c:18:87:74:ad:a1:c3:90:55:af:27:f4:87:0c:4a:bb:5a:0d:
        f1:87:a4:2d:dc:a4:c1:16:c3:02:21:9b:4c:56:61:fe:ce:a1:
        4a:cb:fc:de:92:57:c6:87:63:38:ba:de:56:d6:3a:62:4c:c5:
        cb:41:75:44:61:f5:f7:d9:fa:9f:ab:35:9e:c3:90:96:b1:0b:
        1a:47:b3:4d:2c:15:60:e0:95:ed:98:b4:31:8a:7e:77:f3:41:
        0e:05:91:f4:1e:1d:fd:74:e6:7c:61:b7:16:f6:ec:a9:b7:d1:
        aa:b0:23:e1:42:8a:c5:50:b3:c8:a9:f3:69:d5:49:1e:95:d3:
        21:12:ba:6a:e9:35:f2:c5:74:15:d9:a7:d5:71:47:9a:a3:fe:
        5b:11:14:50:fe:d9:eb:76:f2:21:1e:88:ac:7c:4e:ea:19:f8:
        74:d8:0f:0b:97:af:3c:ce:95:79:b5:6a:b0:67:c0:0c:33:3a:
        fd:32:9d:a1:4c:0b:6e:21:b5:de:c4:e6:2f:6d:07:70:7d:31:
        0c:3f:7d:b6:4d:ac:d7:3e:94:4c:1c:26:a2:19:1e:ee:ff:da:
        73:73:49:38:c0:32:9e:22:8c:ed:d2:1f:3c:50:ba:89:df:d6:
        a5:ab:df:52:a2:79:7f:e0:91:d7:6a:45:44:9a:6a:d3:bc:a0:
        c0:18:ba:c0
-----BEGIN CERTIFICATE-----
MIIEnjCCA4agAwIBAgIBATANBgkqhkiG9w0BAQQFADCBjTELMAkGA1UEBhMCVVMx
CzAJBgNVBAgTAkZMMREwDwYDVQQHEwhIZWF0aHJvdzEPMA0GA1UEChMGVHJpemVu
MREwDwYDVQQLEwhTb2Z0d2FyZTEXMBUGA1UEAxMOd3d3LnRyaXplbi5jb20xITAf
BgkqhkiG9w0BCQEWEnphcmVtYmFAdHJpemVuLmNvbTAeFw0wMTEwMjAwMDAyMDVa
```

```
Fw0wMjEwMjAwMDAyMDVaMHoxCzAJBgNVBAYTAlVTMQswCQYDVQQIEwJGTDEPMA0G
A1UEChMGVHJpemVuMREwDwYDVQQLEwhTb2Z0d2FyZTEXMBUGA1UEAxMOd3d3LnRy
aXplbi5jb20xITAfBgkqhkiG9w0BCQEWEnphcmVtYmFkHJpemVuLmNvbTCCASIw
DQYJKoZIhvcNAQEBBQADggEPADCCAQoCggEBAMpXWoGMdz7rEYtaJTrJHTV/WLZ2
AMPhi/7i/lcmW+qiKg0HYlJ82SBxECgrTBnMDRnOiBVO/Gg30fB8X+Q+ZsHt7s5Q
YfczuDfXWYCrlugfXg7r2PBFbi7hatyb2UuVo7/VtyMFX//9sGrg8hf4v1bPgvA3
CS71f4gy14CVZgDCZJ7pv5ywYs9q5jb3YgDcgYECaYsgJhEmAFXDqToa+brhw38Z
ZhEaT9eAmt1coa8qfrHv0/drG4WobqTARrn3eHydNDtCb7krj+FopuhhE1uG1Arw
yCbk76DfTKuhquyFZrRMyQwkWN9sVoLs/1Nuv+VCMzRhnhMcAOlVgvHnQ20CAwEA
AaOCARkwggEVMAkGA1UdEwQCMAAwLAYJYIZIAYb4QgENBB8WHU9wZW5TU0wgR2Vu
ZXJhdGVkVkIENlcnRpZmljYXRlMB0GA1UdDgQWBBQkmWA4HTAJeAO4N3K9lIBpf8FU
VTCBugYDVR0jBIGyMIGvgBQkmWA4HTAJeAO4N3K9lIBpf8FUVaGBk6SBkDCBjTEL
MAkGA1UEBhMCVVMxCzAJBgNVBAgTAkZMMREwDwYDVQQHEwhIZWF0aHJvdzEPMA0G
A1UEChMGVHJpemVuMREwDwYDVQQLEwhTb2Z0d2FyZTEXMBUGA1UEAxMOd3d3LnRy
aXplbi5jb20xITAfBgkqhkiG9w0BCQEWEnphcmVtYmFkHJpemVuLmNvbYIBADAN
BgkqhkiG9w0BAQQFAAOCAQEAfBiHdK2hw5BVryf0hwxKu1oN8YekLdykwRbDAiGb
TFZh/s6hSsv83pJXxodjOLreVtY6YkzFy0F1RGH199n6n6s1nsOQlrELGkezTSwV
YOCV7Zi0MYp+d/NBDgWR9B4d/XTmfGG3FvbsqbfRqrAj4UKKxVCzyKnzadVJHpXT
IRK6auk18sV0Fdmn1XFHmqP+WxEUUP7Z63byIR6IrHxO6hn4dNgPC5evPM6VebVq
sGfADDM6/TKdoUwLbiG13sTmL20HcH0xDD99tk2s1z6UTBwmohke7v/ac3NJOMAy
niKM7dIfPFC6id/WpavfUqJ5f+CR12pFRJpq07ygwBi6wA==
-----END CERTIFICATE-----
```

If you look in the *index.txt* file in the *c:\CARoot* directory you should see the certificate information as a single line item. If you look in the *serial* file you should see "02" which represents the next certificate index (01 is the above certificate).

You should now distribute this newly created *signedcert.crt* file as the signed certificate. This certificate will work in the OpenSSL environment and will function properly with any application that uses the OpenSSL libraries; however, if you want to install this certificate in Windows then you must make some changes as documented in Adjusting the Certificates for Windows Operating Systems.

Signing Certificate Requests (Being a Certificate Authority)

In the previous example we demonstrated the signing of self signed "dummy" certificates. In this section we will show you how to take a certificate request and sign it with your credentials. Similar to Verisign, or Thawte, you create a certificate request usually from Internet Information Server and send it to them to "sign" and return the signed certificate for your use. Creating a certificate request from IIS is discussed in section **Creating PKCS#12 Certificates in Internet Information Server.** You may optionally issue the following command in the MS-DOS prompt to create a Certificate Signing Request:

```
C:\CARoot>req –newkey rsa:1024 –keyout private\dummy.key –out
        private\dummy.pem –config openssl.cnf
```

Note, that in order to create certificate requests, you have to have a Certificate Authority setup. This is sometimes very tough for those who don't want to be a CA. It is therefore recommended to create them from Internet Information Server. After getting the Certificate Signing Request file (or after creating it) you can issue the following command to sign the certificate:

```
C:\CARoot>ca –in certreq.txt –key private\ca.key –out newcerts\mycert.cer –policy
        policy_anything –config openssl.cnf
```

Note that the only difference between signing self-signed certificates and certificate request are the –ss_cert and –in switches respectively.

Adjusting the Certificates for Windows Operating Systems

Windows does not understand the .pem file as first created by OpenSSL. Windows does understand .crt files. You may have noticed that when you sign a certificate, its contents change, you don't just have the BEGIN CERTIFICATE and END CERTIFICATE you have all the information at the top as well. If you merely change the extension of the .pem file to .crt and then double click the file, Windows will give you an error. You must delete the entire contents of the file except for the data between and including the BEGIN CERTIFICATE and the END CERTIFICATE (similar to the self signed CA certificate above). Go ahead and right mouse click on the newly created signedcert.crt file and open the file with WordPad.

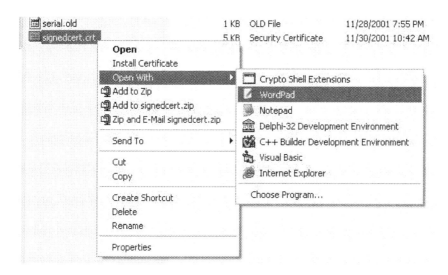

It is best to use WordPad when opening certificate files as NotePad will display all of the extra ASCII character codes and make editing the certificate difficult. Once the file has opened in WordPad, delete everything except for the data between and including the BEGIN CERTIFICATE and the END CERTIFICATE making sure that the BEGIN CERTIFICATE line is the first line and the END CERTIFICATE line is the last line. Save the file (don't worry if you mess up, you can recreate the certificate again, and optionally delete the entry from the index.txt file and serial file). Your file should now look very similar in nature to the ca.crt file.

When you do delete the header information, and then, if necessary, change the extension from .pem to .crt, you can then double click on the file you should see the following noting that your information may be slightly different:

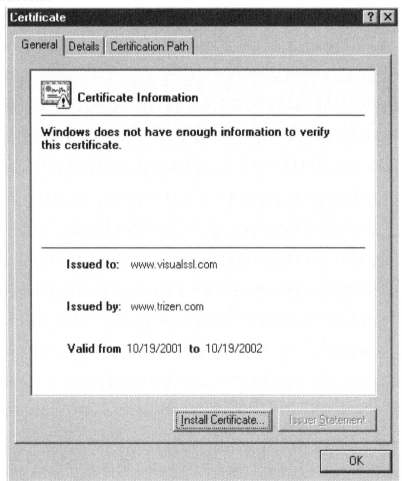

You do have the option of installing the certificate into the Windows certificate database of certificates to trust, but is not necessary at this time. If you check the other tabs, you will notice all of the data you have entered for this signed certificate as well as information about the issuer which is the CA. You will also notice that Windows cannot find any information on this certificate. We will install the CA certificate in the next section.

Installing the CA Certificate into the Windows Operating System

For any signed certificate, you must take out the header information and have only the BEGIN CERTIFICATE and END CERTIFICATE information such as the information presented in the **Creating the CA Certificate** section. Open up the ca.crt file in the *c:\CARoot\private* directory by right mouse clicking on the file and then opening it up with WordPad. Make sure it looks like a standard certificate with no header information just ------BEGIN CERTIFICATE----- and ------END CERTIFICATE ----------.

If the CA certificate conforms with Windows .crt formatting, then you can simply double click on the certificate. When the dialog pops up, similar to the above screen shot, press the *Install Certificate...* button:

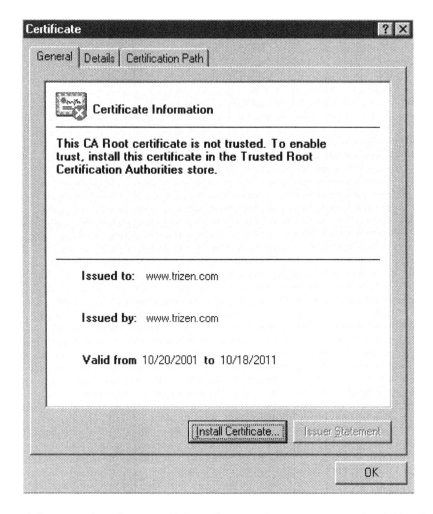

After pressing the *Install Certificate...* button you see the following dialog box:

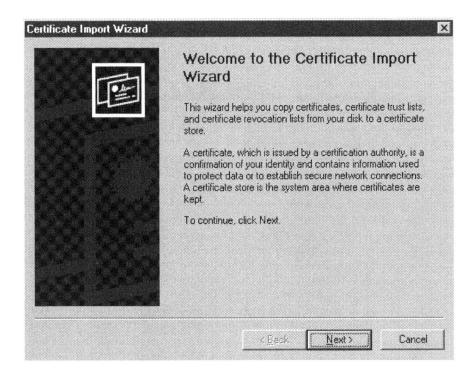

Just Press *Next* > to continue

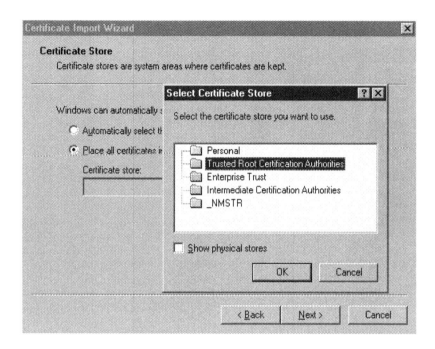

In the above dialog I have selected the *"Place all certificates in the following store"* and then pressed the *Browse...* button. When the Select Certificate Store popped up, I selected the *"Trusted Root Certificate Authorities"* store and pressed *Ok*. Press Next > to continue. You should see the following dialog:

Just Press *Finish...* to complete the process:

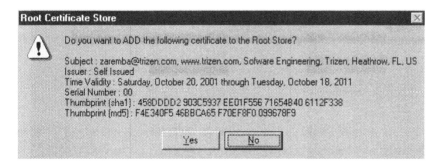

Press *Yes* to continue and install the certificate. You have now installed the CA Root certificate as a trusted Certificate Authority. The next step will be to install any public certificates that have been signed by the CA Root certificate. You may notice something different the next time you double click on the CA certificate (ca.crt):

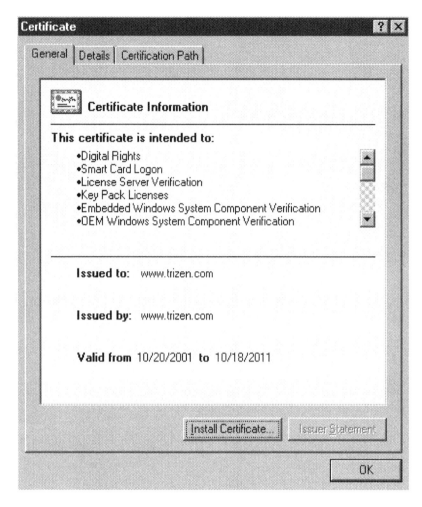

In the above image, Windows now has some information to work with, unlike the first time we double clicked on the CA Certificate. If you then click on the Certification Path tab at the top you will see that Windows now says the certificate path is Ok as well.

At this point create and sign a certificate, and then double click on the .crt file of the newly created signed certificate in the *c:\CARoot\newcerts* directory (you may have to change the name to have a .crt extension and also remove the header information). If you followed the directions in the **Creating a New Public Certificate and Key Pair** then you already have a certificate that you can simply double click on (making sure you made it compatible for windows). You should see the following dialog:

Notice that you have not installed this certificate. It is already trusted, because it's root certificate is trusted which is the CA Certificate that was installed earlier. If you click on the *Certification Path* tab you will see the certificate chain:

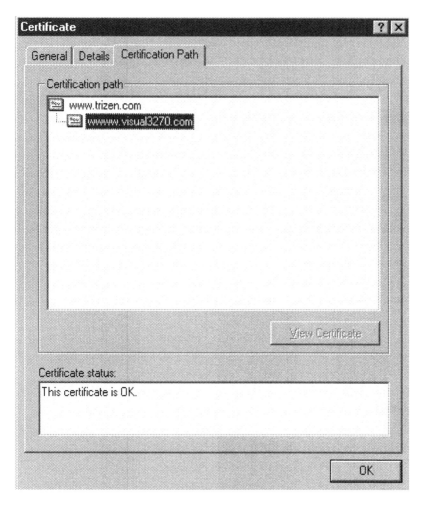

Notice that the Root certificate for this newly created and signed certificate is the www.trizen.com (Common Name) certificate. If you click on this, then you can view the CA certificate.

Using Internet Explorer to Install the Certificate

An alternate way to install certificates is to use Internet Explorer which will allow you to install .pem files (assuming they have been modified to conform to Windows parsing) or any other files that conform to PEM or x509 structure.

Open up Internet Explorer and from the menu bar select Tools | Internet Options. When you select the Content tab you should see the following:

When the above dialog appears (assuming you're using Internet 5.0) click

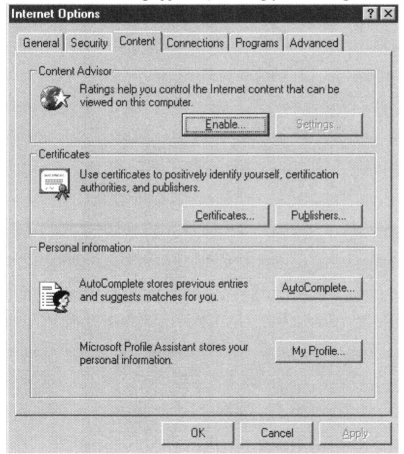

on the *Certificates...* button. You should get the following dialog:

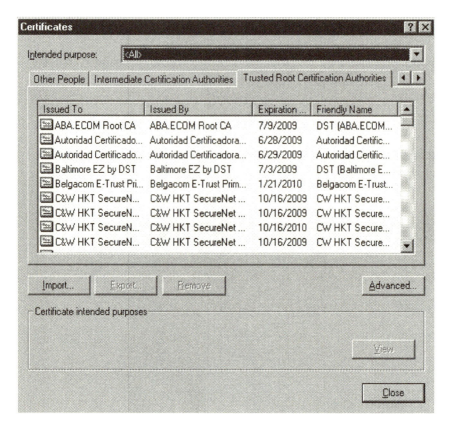

Certificate Chaining

From here you can see all of the Trusted Root Certificates (Certificate Authorities). If one of these CA has signed a certificate that your computer is validating, the root will be accepted. The root certificate is at the top of the chain for any signed certificates. This goes hand in hand with certificate chaining, whereas there can be many Certificate Authorities, each one positioning itself in the certificate chain. In this case Trizen is the Root certificate and any certificates we sign will have a depth of 1 (starting at 0) where position 0 is the signed certificate and position 1 is the Trizen Root. If you are developing secure applications using Visual SSL or OpenSSL then you should review the material on client verification and certificate depths.

Importing the CA Certificate

On the above dialog, press the *Import...* button. You should see the following dialog:

Just press the *Next >* button. You should see the next dialog:

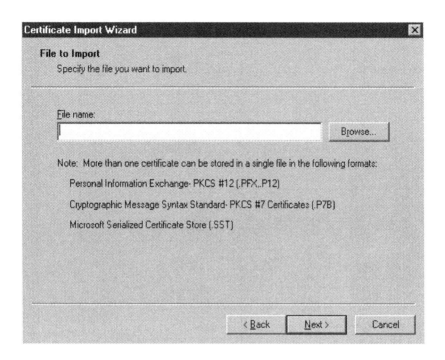

Press the *Browse...* button and navigate to the signed certificate you wish to import *i.e. ca.crt* in the *private* directory of the CARoot folder. You may have to view *.* file types. Press the *Next >* button to continue.

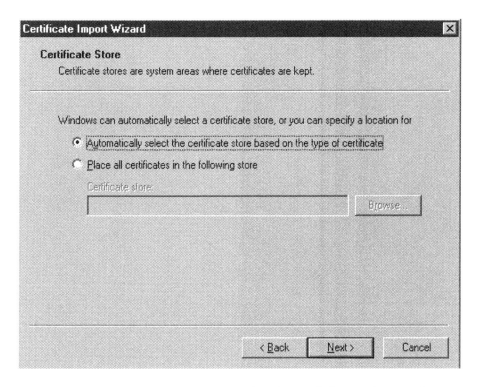

You should just accept the setting in the above dialog and press the *Next >* button. You should see the following dialog.

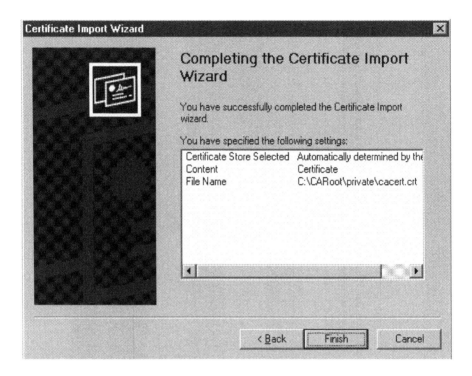

At this point it is the same as if you had double clicked on a .crt file. Remember you can't double click on .pem files and get this dialog, you must either go through Internet Explorer or change the name so that it has a .crt extension—making sure you have removed all the header information and leaving only the ------- BEGIN CERTIFICATE ----- and the -------- END CERTIFICATE ------- data.

Using the OpenSSL Applications s_server.exe & s_client.exe

Undoubtedly you will want to test your certificates. OpenSSL provides you with a rich set of applications that can be found in the *c:\OpenSSL\openssl-0.9.6a\out32dll\release* directory. We have already discussed several of them in the above sections, but as a developer you will want to use some of the other applications to test your own SSL enabled applications. Remember that these utilities are all MS-DOS based and it is recommended that you place a copy of command.com or cmd.exe (for NT) in the *c:\OpenSSL\openssl-0.9.6a\out32dll\release* directory.

Running s_client.exe and s_server.exe

We can guarantee that you will use s_server.exe at some point during your SSL development life cycle. This is a great utility that will test your client's capabilities and ensure that you are communicating properly. If your client can communicate with s_server.exe then you can be pretty sure it will perform accurately and appropriately with other SSL enabled servers including https://www.verisign.com and others.

Copy the *server.pem* and *client.pem* files from the C:\OpensSSL\openssl-0.9.6a\apps directory to the C:\OpenSSL\openssl-0.9.6a\out32dll\release directory.
Double click on your command.com or cmd.exe file in the *release* directory. When the command window pops up, type the following at the command prompt:

C:\OpenSSL\openssl-0.9.6a\out32dll\release>*s_server –accept 4433*

```
C:\OpenSSL\openssl-0.9.6a\cmd.exe - s_server -accept 4433

C:\OpenSSL\openssl-0.9.6a\out32dll\Release>s_server -ac
cept 4433
Loading 'screen' into random state - done
Using default temp DH parameters
ACCEPT
```

The s_server.exe application is now ready to accept clients. At this point, stop the server by pressing Ctrl+C twice to exit the application. Type in the following at the command prompt and press enter:

C:\OpenSSL\openssl-0.9.6a\out32dll\release>*s_server -help*

This will bring up all of the options that can be utilized with the s_server.exe application. If you use none of the options the server will accept on port 4433 using server.pem as the certificate which will also contain the private key. Note that you can place the private key into the same file as the public certificate when using OpenSSL.

If you haven't already stopped the execution of the s_server.exe application, just press Ctrl and the letter C twice while still holding the Control key. At this point copy the ca.key and the ca.crt file to this *release* directory (from CARoot\private). Then at the command prompt type the following:

C:\OpenSSL\openssl-0.9.6a\out32dll\release>*s_server -cert ca.crt -key ca.key*

This will start the s_server application with the CA Public Certificate and CA Private Key files that were created earlier. If it asks for the PEM password, just type in the password that you made when you created the CA Key file.

At this point, let the s_server.exe continue to run and double click on the command.com or cmd.exe (for NT) file to bring up a new MS-DOS prompt. At the DOS prompt type the following:

C:\OpenSSL\openssl-0.9.6a\out32dll\release>*s_client—cert ca.crt —key ca.key*

You should see the following:

```
C:\OpenSSL\openssl-0.9.6a\cmd.exe - s_client -cert ca.crt...

No client certificate CA names sent

SSL handshake has read 1655 bytes and written 256 bytes

New, TLSv1/SSLv3, Cipher is EDH-RSA-DES-CBC3-SHA
Server public key is 2048 bit
SSL-Session:
        Protocol  : TLSv1
        Cipher    : EDH-RSA-DES-CBC3-SHA
        Session-ID: 363777F1CEFF42F21767002FF543ABC4790FA25
AECAF5EEDD7E1ECE86F925B36
        Session-ID-ctx:
        Master-Key: 5F13D23E24384251B7AFA7EC607C5539D2FA63B
F7ED0A4E7E4245283A38D065EF4410A7D8511276A4F7DE71BCD0F3D
24
        Key-Arg   : None
        Start Time: 1167325488
        Timeout   : 300 (sec)
        Verify return code: 18 (self signed certificate)
```

If you did not see this make sure you have placed the *ca.crt* and *ca.key* file into the same directory as the *s_client.exe* application (c:\OpenSSL\openssl-0.9.6a\out32dll\release). Also, you may want to add the switch *—connect 127.0.0.1:4433* which represents the host IP and Port number of the *s_server.exe* application.

Notice the last line: Verify return code: 18 (self signed certificate). Which makes sense, the s_client.exe application will automatically attempt to verify the server's certificate, which in the case of the s_server.exe application we are using the CA certificate which was self signed! At this point shutdown your s_client.exe application and then the s_server.exe application.

Copy the <u>signed</u> certificate signedcert.crt created earlier (signedcert.crt) file (or whatever it is named in the *C:\CARoot* directory) to the *C:\OpenSSL\openssl-0.9.6a\out32dll\release* directory. Copy the cert.key which was used to create the request certificate, then later signed —this is the public key pair (actually there are three, a publicly signed certificate, a request certificate and a key file). Type in the following into one of the MD-DOS window command prompts:

C:\OpenSSL\openssl-0.9.6a\out32dll\release>*s_server –cert signedcert.crt –key cert.key*

Your server should be up and running. At another MS-DOS prompt (open another window if necessary) type in the following:

C:\OpenSSL\openssl-0.9.6a\out32dll\release>*s_client –cert signedcert.crt –key cert.key*

If all has gone well then you should get another verification error? At least you're not getting the self signed certificate error "18" but is error "21" any better? This error represents the problem of not being able to validate a server's certificate using a Trusted Certificate Store (such as that created when installing certificates in Windows above).

This has everything to do with the client's verification process. Basically we need to inform the s_client.exe application that it should look in a file for those certificates that it should trust! This is accomplished by using the –CAFile switch. Stop running the s_client.exe application but **keep the s_server application running**.

Creating a CAFile

A CAFile is very easy to create and consists of nothing more than a bunch of public certificates appended to each other. To create a CAFile, from windows right mouse click on the Start button. Select the Explore pop up menu item. When the explorer window pops up navigate to *c:\OpenSSL\openssl-0.9.6a\out32dll\release*. In the right hand pane, right mouse click in the area where the release files are located, selecting New | Text Document. It should now appear in the right pane awaiting for you to give it a name. Rename the file root.pem. Your directory should look like the following:

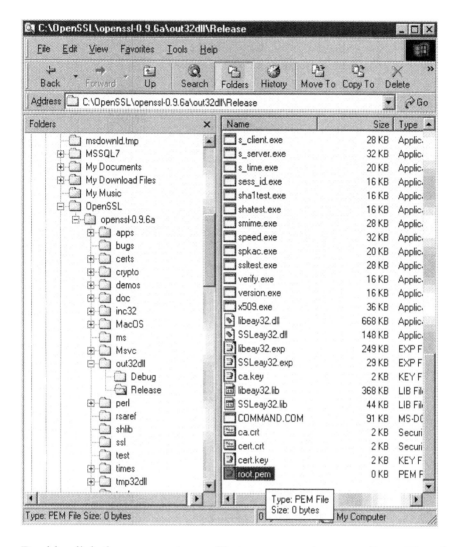

Double click the new root.pem file to open up the text editor. You should have a blank file. Next, right mouse click on the signedcert.crt file and select Open With and either select WordPad if its available or select Choose Program and use the WordPad program. When WordPad opens up, select all the text (Edit | Select All) in the signedcert.crt file between and include BEGIN CERTIFICATE and END CERTIFICATE and then copy the selection to the clipboard (Edit | Copy):

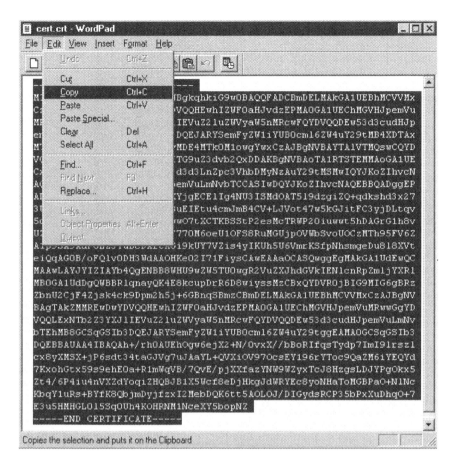

Now go to the other WordPad application which represents the blank root.pem file and paste this data into that file then save the file and exit. You have successfully created a CAFile. If you have not already closed the s_client.exe application do so now, then at the command prompt type the following:

C:\OpenSSL\openssl-0.9.6a\out32dll\release>*s_client –cert signedcert.crt –key cert.key –CAfile root.pem*

If all goes well, you should see the same error! "Unable to verify the first certificate" is not what you would probably expect, but we have only copied the signed certificate, we still have to copy the CA certificate (ca.crt). Shutdown the s_client.exe application and copy the ca.crt certificate data to the bottom of the root.pem file using the same method as above. The root.pem file should now look something similar to the following:

```
-----BEGIN CERTIFICATE-----
MIIExzCCA6+gAwIBAgIBBzANBgkqhkiG9w0BAQQFADCBmDELMAkGA1UEBhMCVVMx
CzAJBgNVBAgTAkZMMREwDwYDVQQHEwhIZWF0aHJvdzEPMA0GA1UEChMGVHJpemVu
MRwwGgYDVQQLExNTb2Z3YXJlIEVuZ2luZWVyaW5nMRcwFQYDVQQDEw53d3cudHJp
emVuLmNvbTEhMB8GCSqGSIb3DQEJARYSemFyZW1iYUB0cml6ZW4uY29tMB4XDTAx
MTAyMDE4MTk0M1oXDTAyMTAyMDE4MTk0M1owgYwxCzAJBgNVBAYTAlVTMQswCQYD
VQQIEwJGTDERMA8GA1UEBxMITG9uZ3dvb2QxDDAKBgNVBAoTA1RTTEMMAoGA1UE
CxMDRU5HMRwwGgYDVQQDExN3d3d3Lnzpc3VhbDMyNzAuY29tMSMwIQYJKoZIhvcN
AQkBFhRyZWxhdGlvbnNAdHJpemVuLmNvbTCCASIwDQYJKoZIhvcNAQEBBQADggEP
ADCCAQoCggEBAMduDyCEUL3XYjgECElIg4NU3ISMdOAT5l9dzgiZQ+qdkshd3x27
3WeCq+esdeBs3dYYOEPfpxkBuEIEtu4cmJmB4CV+LJVot47w5kGJitFC3yjDLtqv
5q/PcT/vKf5jb2DA+iw7KlOwwO7tXCTKBSStP2esMcTRWP20iuwwt5hDAGrGlh8v
UZMQdxM93nFAhf5RkrYc1plF770M6oeU1OFS8RuMGUjpOVWbSvoUOCzMTh95FV6Z
Alp9SA9AdPGLz3TuBcDAftXGi9kUY7VZis4yIKUh5U6VmrKSfpNhsmgeDu8l8XVt
eiQqAG0B/oFQlv0DH3WdAAOHKe02I7l1FiysCAwEAAaOCASQwggEgMAkGA1UdEwQC
MAAwLAYJYIZIAYb4QgENBB8WHU9wZW5TU0wgR2VuZXJhdGVkIENlcnRpZmljYXRl
MB0GA1UdDgQWBBRlqnayQK4E8kcupDrR6D8wiyssMzCBxQYDVR0jBIG9MIG6gBRz
ZbnU2CjF4Zjsk4ck9Dpm2h5j+6GBnqSBmzCBmDELMAkGA1UEBhMCVVMxCzAJBgNV
BAgTAkZMMREwDwYDVQQHEwhIZWF0aHJvdzEPMA0GA1UEChMGVHJpemVuMRwwGgYD
VQQLExNTb2Z3YXJlIEVuZ2luZWVyaW5nMRcwFQYDVQQDEw53d3cudHJpemVuLmNv
bTEhMB8GCSqGSIb3DQEJARYSemFyZW1iYUB0cml6ZW4uY29tggEAMA0GCSqGSIb3
DQEBBAUAA4IBAQAh+/rh0AUEhOgw6ejX2+N/0vxX//bBoRIfqsTydp7ImI9lrszl
cx8yXMSX+jP6sdt34taGJVg7uJAaYL+QVXiOV97OcsEY196rYToc9QaZM6iYEQYd
7KxohGtx59s9ehE0a+RlmWqVB/7QvE/pjXXfazYNW9WZyxTcJ8HzgsLDJYPgOkx5
Zt4/6P4iu4nVXZdYoqiZHQBJB1X5Wcf8eDjHkgJdWRYEc8yoNHaToMGBPaO+NlNc
KbqY1uRs+BYfK8QbjmDyjfzxI2MebDQK6tt5AOLOJ/DIGydsRCP35bPxXuDhqO+7
E3u5HMHGL015Sq0Uh4KOHRNM1NceXY5bopNZ
-----END CERTIFICATE-----
-----BEGIN CERTIFICATE-----
MIIEpjCCA46gAwIBAgIBADANBgkqhkiG9w0BAQQFADCBmDELMAkGA1UEBhMCVVMx
CzAJBgNVBAgTAkZMMREwDwYDVQQHEwhIZWF0aHJvdzEPMA0GA1UEChMGVHJpemVu
MRwwGgYDVQQLExNTb2Z3YXJlIEVuZ2luZWVyaW5nMRcwFQYDVQQDEw53d3cudHJp
emVuLmNvbTEhMB8GCSqGSIb3DQEJARYSemFyZW1iYUB0cml6ZW4uY29tMB4XDTAx
MTAyMDE1NDkxM1oXDTExMTAxODE1NDkxM1owgZxCzAJBgNVBAYTAlVTMQswCQYD
VQQIEwJGTDERMA8GA1UEBxMISGVhdGhyb3cxDzANBgNVBAoTBlRyaXplbjEcMBoG
A1UECxMTU29md2FyZSBFbmdpbmVlcmluuZEXMBUGA1UEAxMOd3d3LnRyaXplbi5j
b20xITAfBgkqhkiG9w0BCQEWEnphcmVtYmFAdHJpemVuLmNvbTCCASIwDQYJKoZI
hvcNAQEBBQADggEPADCCAQoCggEBALPCypLQBuw53sRHHKuNK557iu6tibDcIKZZ
mYCal7Sww8Jd0gdLYGAFxJ5l0PwJZVxILUbbAiUCw2jQFPjq856HaxZ6s6smwWTZ
7piILEmbE46eKoTLkUybL3pwg43DuU6Zoizon+zNT1jwSoFGs1MMs3JdYhkuoGe8
kCF2KxRMxyY+o+RmdjSx158zG0S5yssSn2bbOjCeZzccRzQienVvZYbVahW3wrA8
j/oQubRhROD1jyDJRuDnZ+DvhhLxP0bdM11eUg9QQtl/ftYttL+RcgdORDB1GGV5
ELu79ukA/2UFh7QoZaBXZdje+uo2kITb97FKtjSMOrDOn/35GQECAwEAAaOB+DCB
9TAdBgNVHQ4EFgQUc2W51NgoxeGY7JOHJPQ6ZtoeY/swgcUGA1UdIwSBvTCBuoAU
c2W51NgoxeGY7JOHJPQ6ZtoeY/uhgZ6kgZswgZxCzAJBgNVBAYTAlVTMQswCQYD
VQQIEwJGTDERMA8GA1UEBxMISGVhdGhyb3cxDzANBgNVBAoTBlRyaXplbjEcMBoG
A1UECxMTU29md2FyZSBFbmdpbmVlcmluuZEXMBUGA1UEAxMOd3d3LnRyaXplbi5j
b20xITAfBgkqhkiG9w0BCQEWEnphcmVtYmFAdHJpemVuLmNvbYIBADAMBgNVHRME
BTADAQH/MA0GCSqGSIb3DQEBBAUAA4IBAQAX41RvA0Q+jluqo2o5Tym4/BO6NSR2
zaeAoOOnT8Sd+QHLNXpdC/Wz53tFgp1Kvkx9hwi+/wF082arpYMFaC63vSExl9v/
JMTiTiLcc0yC8z4XXVmgTr4CDRXurpTb4Zk6byeTxOn2pxXWFeOsEB/qIFHq+WDe
```

```
6QXizsMZ2YO60+cP7QAfsEnW5HIf8NOS6+KM6gbkWSgYpkZz5BeSidIDOilRSaEF
R4Yuox83E5RzcJ6xNOJzSD5AxvkRenhMLg7p59n/o8/JoASRg6ihovhs+UEXj6Z2
v+DdhwRuE/nLv5qt52jwUUj+zq1Wcinryb4QIErNaoPqlr2SyCkMlA4U
-----END CERTIFICATE-----
```

At this point you can go to the MS-DOS prompt where you stopped the s_client.exe application and press the up-arrow until you see the previous command. If this does not work just type in the previous command and press enter. You should see the following:

Notice *"Verify return code: 0 (ok)"* response for the client verification! This is what we wanted from the beginning. So did we need the cert.crt certificate in the root.pem? The answer is no, as long as you have the top level certificate installed in the CAFile (root.pem) the client will return "ok."

59

OpenSSL Utilities

S SERVER

s_server is a great tool for testing your SSL client applications; however, it only handles one request at a time, so if you're interested in testing your applications against an SSL server then purchase Visual SSL for ActiveX, Delphi, or C++Builder which has a multi-threaded blocking server and an Asynchronous non-blocking server and source code to match. The following selected "switches" are available for use within s_server. An example follows each switch.

-accept [port]

> The TCP port the server should "listen" on. The default is 4433. The next line will start a server listening on port 3000.
> *s_server –accept 3000*

-cert [certname]

> This is the public certificate to use and can be a physical path to the certificate. Note that if you use a DSS cipher suite then you must use a DSS certificate as well as the matching private key file (see GENDSA). If a certificate is not specified then the server will attempt to load server.pem in the local directory. If the public and private key do not match the server will exit. Developers should note that if a DSS certificate is specified then only DSS clients will be accepted and is the same for RSA certificates and RSA clients.
> *s_server –accept 3000 –cert c:\CARoot\private\ca.crt*

-key [keyfile]

> This is the private key file to use and can be a physical path to the certificate. If no key file is presented then the server will attempt to load the key from the certificate file (key file data and certificate data can exist in the same file). If no key data can be found the server will attempt to load "server.pem." Developers should provide their own public and key files as described above. Servers

must have a public and private key file and it is preferred to encrypt the key file as described earlier. Notice you can use complete paths or relative paths.

s_server –key c:\CARoot\private\ca.key –cert c:\CARoot\private\ca.crt

-no_tmp_rsa

Some export (EXP) cipher suites generate a temporary RSA key. By setting this option no temporary RSA key will be created. Consequently, a client that only supports EXP type cipher suites may fail the handshake and not be able to connect. Developers, when using client connections should try to connect first with a US domestic cipher.

s_server –no_tmp_rsa –accept 3000 –cert ca.crt –key ca.key

-verify [depth], -Verify [depth]

As discussed earlier, a client's certificate can be requested by the server for verification. By using the **–verify** [value] the client's certificate is requested with a certificate chain depth specified by [value] but will not shutdown if the client doesn't present a certificate. The **–Verify** [depth] switch is the same as the lowercase version but will shutdown the connection if the certificate is not presented for verification. As mentioned earlier, the certificate chain represents the number of Certificate Authorities that have "signed" the certificate and then the actual issued certificate. By setting the [depth] integer value, developers can set the maximum number of CA's that are in the chain including the issued certificate. Most certificate chains will have 1 or 2 CA's.

s_server –Verify 1 –cert ca.pem –key key.pem –accept 2000

-CApath [directory]

This switch represents a directory where the acceptable certificates are kept, usually within a CA directory structure. The important thing to note is this directory must have the **perl** script utility **c_rehash** (in tools directory of OpenSSL) run regularly on the

certificates in the directory. It is easier for Windows developers to utilize the **–CAFile** [file] switch.
s_server –Verify 1 –CAPath c:\CARoot\certs

-CAfile [file]

This switch points to the file that contains a list of all acceptable certificates and acceptable Certificate Authorities. See earlier discussion on client verification on how to create this file.
s_server –CAFile c:\CARoot\root.pem

-state

This option will display each SSL protocol step in the handshake upon the acceptance of a client connection.
s_server –state –accept 4433 –cert ca.crt –key ca.key

-debug

selecting this option/switch will produce an exorbitant amount of information on the client connection including a hex dump. This option is best if analyzing the entire protocol from start to finish and is best used with NT's cmd.exe DOS prompt.
s_server –debug –accept 4433 –no_tmp_rsa

-nbio

This switch turns on non-blocking connections which don't block execution until a read/write is performed. Non-blocking connections are usually associated with asynchronous event notification and are used primarily for non serialized connections such as a chat program. Non-blocking connections continuously call Accept until the client connection is accepted.
s_server –accept 4000 –nbio

-quiet

This is basically the opposite of any "debug" switches turning all reporting of the client connections off.
s_server –accept 3000 –quiet

-ssl2, -ssl3, -tls1, -no_ssl2, -no_ssl3, -no_tls1

These switches disable or enable the use of certain SSL or TLS protocols. For example, the –ssl3 switch will force only SSL version 3 connections. SSL version 3 is probably the most widespread with respect to new technologies and should be used most of the time. The TLSv1 is basically the same as SSL version 3 and is gaining acceptance rapidly.

s_server –accept 3000 –ssl3

-bugs

This switch will enable workarounds for known SSL or TLS bugs.

s_server –bugs

-cipher [cipherlist]

This option will set the server's acceptable ciphers. If not specified, the server will default to accepting any of the available ciphers in the OpenSSL library; however, you may want to test a server or client's ability or inability to find a "shared cipher." If utilized, upon the client's initial connection the first matching pair between the client and server (using the client's list) will be selected. If the server does not support any of the client's preferred ciphers, the connection will be closed with "no shared ciphers." Acceptable ciphers should be "colon" delimited.

s_server –accept 443 –cipher EXP-RC4-MD5:RC4-MD5

-www

Use this option to check a web browser's connection to the server. The server will return the connection information back to the web browser in HTML format. After starting the server using an RSA certificate, developers can enter https://127.0.0.1:4433 into the browser to see the connection information returned from the server assuming the server and the web browser are on the same machine.

s_server –accept 4433 –www

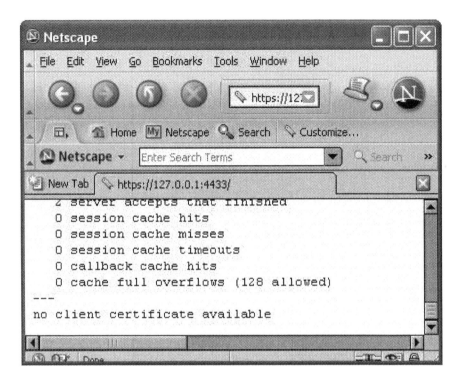

```
2 server accepts that finished
0 session cache hits
0 session cache misses
0 session cache timeouts
0 callback cache hits
0 cache full overflows (128 allowed)
---
no client certificate available
```

You may get some unusual errors if you have a really secure web browser, so this may not work on more modern web browsers without adding the certificate to the brower's list of approved certificates.

-WWW

This switch will emulate a web server and return the request page if it exists in the server's executable directory. For instance if http://127.0.0.1:4433/page.html is requested, then page.html will be returned if it exists in the server's executable directory. Developers should make sure that the file first exists before making this test.

-rand [file(s)]

This switch specifies the location of a file that has random data within it or multiple files that can be used to seed the random number generator. If multiple files are specified then Windows users must use a ";" semicolon delimiter. It has been reported that

hacking can be achieved by generating the same random number and it is recommended to use something such as a bit map file.
s_server –accept 443 –cert cert.pem –key key.pem –rand .rnd

s_server runtime commands

These commands can be entered into your server during its execution:

Key	Description
Q	By entering a single 'q' this will end the current SSL connection.
Q	Enter this to close the current connection and exit the server.
R	This will renegotiate the SSL client connection.
R	This will renegotiate the SSL client connection and request the client's certificate.
P	send some plain text down the underlying TCP connection: this should cause the client to disconnect due to a protocol violation.
S	print out some session cache status information

S_CLIENT

s_client is a great utility for testing your SSL servers and has a number of options that will make debugging your applications a little easier. The following selected switches will help you make your applications SSL compliant:

-connect [host:port]

This switch is used to connect to the specified host. If no host is specified then the client will default to 127.0.0.1 port 4433.
s_client –connect 127.0.0.1:4433 –cert ca.crt –key ca.key

-cert [cert file]

This will specify the public certificate to use during an SSL handshake. This is only needed if the server requests a client's certificate. It should be noted that most http servers do not request a certificate and as such the default for s_client is no certificate.
s_client –connect 127.0.0.1:4433 –cert cert.pem –key cert.key

-key [keyfile]

Like the s_server –key switch, this switch will load the private key file. If no key file is used the client application will attempt to use the public certificate. If the public certificate does not contain any private key information then client will not use a certificate.
s_client –connect 127.0.0.1:4433 –cert ca.crt –key ca.key

-verify [depth]

This specified the server's certificate chain depth to use and turns on the server certificate verification process. The [depth] specifies the maximum number of CA's that can be present in the server's certificate chain, which will usually be 1 or 2. Even if a server's certificate fails the verification process, the connection is still made. In order to verify the certificate completely developers must also use the CAFile switch to load the CA's that are trusted and the associated certificates to trust in order to get a complete Ok from the verification process as discussed earlier.

s_client –connect 127.0.0.1:3000 –verify 2 –cert c:\CARoot\cert.pem

-CApath [directory]

This switch represents a directory where the acceptable server certificates are kept, usually within a CA directory structure. The important thing to note is this directory must have the **perl** script utility **c_rehash**(in tools directory of OpenSSL) run regularly on the certificates in the directory. It is easier for Windows developers to utilize the **–CAFile** [file] switch.

s_client –verify 2 –CAPath c:\CARoot\certs.

-CAfile [file]

This switch points to the file that contains a list of all the acceptable server certificates and acceptable Certificate Authorities. See earlier discussion on client verification on how to create this file.

s_client –CAFile c:\CARoot\root.pem

-reconnect

This switch will connect to the server 5 consecutive times and is useful for minor stress testing and session cache testing.

s_client –reconnect –connect 127.0.0.1:443

-showcerts

This will display the complete server certificate chain. Normal connection will only show the server's certificate information.

s_client –connect 127.0.0.1:3000 –showcerts

-state

This option will display each SSL protocol step in the handshake upon the acceptance of a client connection.

s_client –state –connect 127.0.0.1:4433 –cert ca.crt –key ca.key

-debug

Selecting this option/switch will produce an exorbitant amount of information on the server connection including a hex dump. This

option is best if analyzing the entire protocol from start to finish and is best used with NT's cmd.exe DOS prompt.
s_client –debug –connect 127.0.0.1:4433

-nbio

This switch turns on the non-blocking connection type, which doesn't block execution while waiting for a read/write. Non blocking connections are usually associated with asynchronous event notification and are used primarily for non serialized connections such as a chat program. Non-blocking connections continuously call Accept until the client connection is accepted.
s_client –connect 127.0.0.1:4000 –nbio

-quiet

This is basically the opposite of any "debug" switches turning all reporting of the client connections off.
s_client –connect 127.0.0.1:3000 –quiet

-ssl2, -ssl3, -tls1, -no_ssl2, -no_ssl3, -no_tls1

These switches disable or enable the use of certain SSL or TLS protocols. For example, the –ssl3 switch will force only SSL version 3 connections. SSL version 3 is probably the most widespread with respect to new technologies and should be used most of the time. The TLSv1 is basically the same as SSL version 3 and is gaining acceptance rapidly.
s_client –accept 3000 –ssl3

-bugs

This switch will enable workarounds for known SSL or TLS bugs.
s_client –bugs

-cipher [cipherlist]

This option will set the client's preferred ciphers in order of preference. If not specified, the client will default to presenting any of the available ciphers in the OpenSSL library; however, you may want to test a server or client's ability or inability to find a "shared cipher." If utilized, upon the client's initial connection the

first matching pair between the client and server (using the client's list) will be selected. If the server does not support any of the client's preferred ciphers, the connection will be closed with "no shared ciphers." Acceptable ciphers should be "colon" delimited.
s_client –connect 127.0.0.1:443 –cipher EXP-RC4-MD5:RC4-MD5

-rand [file(s)]

This switch specifies the location of a file that has random data within it or multiple files that can be used to seed the random number generator. If multiple files are specified then Windows users must use a ";" semicolon delimiter. It has been reported that hacking an encrypted session can be achieved by generating the same random number and it is recommended to use something such as a bit map file.
s_client –connect 127.0.0.1:443 –cert cert.pem –key key.pem – rand .rnd

ASN1PARSE

The ASN1Parse utility will take either a PEM (Privacy Enhanced Mail RFC1422) or DER (Distinguished Encoding Rules) public certificate and parse the certificate information, displaying the information. The PEM format consists of the DER base64 encoding while the standard DER format is compatible with RFC2459; both of which are based on the ASN.1 (Abstract Syntax Notation 1) and include X.509 information as well. There are several options that can be used but the most useful are as follows:

-in [certificate]

This options specifies the certificate file. The default certificate format is PEM and as such the –inform and –in file must match.

-inform [PEM | DER]

This option sets the type of file that will be parsed.

asn1parse –in ca.pem –inform PEM

DSAPARAM

This utility is useful for generating DSA parameter files. DSA, as opposed to RSA, utilizes the Digital Signature Algorithm now known as the Digital Signature Standard (DSS) and can only use SHA-1 whereas RSA can utilize SHA-1 and MD5 digest algorithms. It is really only important to know that a DSA/DSS client cannot communicate with an RSA server. There is really only one reason to use this utility and it is to create the DSA parameter file, which can then be used to create a DSA key pair.

-out [file]

This specifies the out file that will have the DSA parameters. The out file will default to a PEM format unless DER is specified in the –outform.

-outform [PEM | DER]

This switch specifies the type of out file to create.

[number]

This is not a switch but a parameter and represents the number of bits to use when generating the parameters. This must be the last parameter in the command.

-rand [file(s)]

This switch specifies the location of a file that has random data within it or multiple files that can be used to seed the random number generator. If multiple files are specified then Windows users must use a ";" semicolon delimiter. It has been reported that hacking an encrypted session can be achieved by generating the same random number and it is recommended to use something such as a bit map file or a privately used file that has random data.

dsaparam –outform PEM –out dsaparams.pem –rand .rnd 512

GENDSA

This utility will generate a DSA (Digital Signature Algorithm) key from a DH parameters file that has been created using the DSAPARAM utility.

-out [file]

This specifies the out file name of the DSA generated private key file.

-des, -des3, -idea

This switches/options represent the encryption format for the key. To encrypt the key select one of the above algorithms or leave the key file unencrypted. This will prompt the user for a password.

-rand [file(s)]

This switch specifies the location of a file that has random data within it or multiple files that can be used to seed the random number generator. If multiple files are specified then Windows users must use a ";" semicolon delimiter. It has been reported that hacking an encrypted session can be achieved by generating the same random number and it is recommended to use something such as a bit map file or a privately used file that has random data.

dsaparam-file

A command line parameter rather than a switch, this selects the DSA parameters file to use when generating the DSA key. The DSA parameters file be created using the DSAPARAM utility.

gendsa –out dsa.key –des3 –rand c:\private\.rnd dsaparam.pem

RAND

This utility will generate a random byte file for use with the –rand switch in most of the OpenSSL applications. Many times it is just as good to use a file such as a picture, or word document to seed the random number generator during the openssl commands; however, for simplicity it may be easier to always use the same random bytes file.

-out [file]
This sets the file to create which will have the random bytes. In the OpenSSL documentation and for Certificate Authority management, this file typically consists of only the extension .rnd.

-rand [file(s)]
This switch specifies the location of a file that has random data within it or multiple files that can be used to seed the random number generator. If multiple files are specified then Windows users must use a ";" semicolon delimiter. It has been reported that hacking an encrypted session can be achieved by generating the same random number and it is recommended to use something such as a bit map file or a privately used file that has random data.
[num]
This parameter, rather than a switch, sets the number of random bytes to create and place into the file. It is recommended to have this file at least 1K or 1024 bytes.

C:\>rand –out .rnd 1024

Windows developers should note that usually the only way to open a .rnd file is to edit the file from within a DOS prompt by using the *edit .rnd* command.

VERIFY
This utility will verify the presented certificate similar to the certificate verification process that occurs during the SSL handshake where a client and server both verify each other if requested. Developers can use this utility to extract the code from the verification process as outlined below:

-CAFile [file]
This parameter is the CAFile to use when building the certificate chain. The chain built up by starting with the selected certificate and ending with the CARoot. A certificate is self signed if the

certificate and certificate root are the same. If a match between the certificate and the CAFile is found, then the certificate if verified ok.

[certificate1 certificate2 .. certificateN]
This specifies the certificates to validate/verify.

C:\>OpenSSL verify –CAfile c:\CARoot\root.pem c:\CARoot\newcert.crt

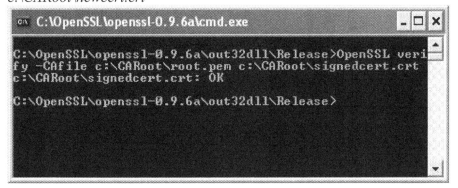

Notice that the return value was OK. This means the certificate returned a verify result of zero (0). If you have followed the examples for creating a certificate and adding your CA root certificate to the root.pem file specified above then you should have similar results. Another possible result could be the following:

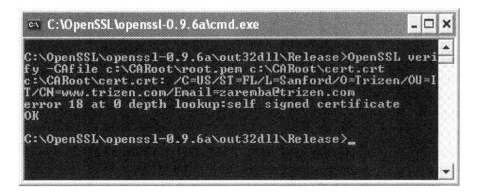

73

In this example, we have selected to verify a certificate that was generated from a key whose public certificate is NOT in the root.pem file and has not been signed. This error is typical of "dummy" certificates, created but not signed. Other errors may be a certificate that has been signed, but the issuer is not in the root.pem CAfile specification.

The following represents the possible errors, defined by the OpenSSL API, that can be received during the verification process and in fact can be seen in the Visual SSL event OnVerifyError:

#	Defined	Long Description
0	X509_V_OK	The operation was successful.
2	X509_V_ERR_UNABLE_TO_GET_ISSUER_CERT	The issuer certificate could not be found: this occurs if the issuer certificate of an untrusted certificate cannot be found.
3	X509_V_ERR_UNABLE_TO_GET_CRL	The CRL of a certificate could not be found. Unused.
4	X509_V_ERR_UNABLE_TO_DECRYPT_CERT_SIGNATURE	the certificate signature could not be decrypted. This means that the actual signature value could not be determined rather than it not matching the expected value, this is only meaningful for RSA keys.
5	X509_V_ERR_UNABLE_TO_DECRYPT_CRL_SIGNATURE	The CRL signature could not be decrypted: this means that the actual signature value could not be determined rather than it not matching the expected value. Unused.
6	X509_V_ERR_UNABLE_TO_DECODE_ISSUER_PUBLIC_KEY	The public key in the certificate SubjectPublicKeyInfo could not be read.
7	X509_V_ERR_CERT_SIGNATURE_FAILURE	The signature of the certificate is invalid.
8	X509_V_ERR_CRL_SIGNATURE_FAILURE	The signature of the certificate is invalid. Unused.
9	X509_V_ERR_CERT_NOT_YET_VALID	The certificate is not yet valid: the notBefore date is after the current time.
10	X509_V_ERR_CRL_NOT_YET_VALID	The CRL is not yet valid. Unused.
11	X509_V_ERR_CERT_HAS_EXPIRED	The certificate has expired: that is the notAfter date is before the current time.
12	X509_V_ERR_CRL_HAS_EXPIRED	The CRL has expired. Unused.
13	X509_V_ERR_ERROR_IN_CERT_NOT_BEFORE_FIELD	the certificate notBefore field contains an invalid time.
14	X509_V_ERR_ERROR_IN_CERT_NOT_AFTER_FIELD	the certificate notAfter field contains an invalid time.
15	X509_V_ERR_ERROR_IN_CRL_LAST_UPDATE_FIELD	the CRL lastUpdate field contains an invalid time. Unused.

16	X509_V_ERR_ERROR_IN_CRL_NEXT_U PDATE_FIELD	the CRL nextUpdate field contains an invalid time. Unused.
17	X509_V_ERR_OUT_OF_MEM	an error occurred trying to allocate memory. This should never happen.
18	X509_V_ERR_DEPTH_ZERO_SELF_SIG NED_CERT	the passed certificate is self signed and the same certificate cannot be found in the list of trusted certificates.
19	X509_V_ERR_SELF_SIGNED_CERT_IN _CHAIN	the certificate chain could be built up using the untrusted certificates but the root could not be found locally.
20	X509_V_ERR_UNABLE_TO_GET_ISSUE R_CERT_LOCALLY	the issuer certificate of a locally looked up certificate could not be found. This normally means the list of trusted certificates is not complete.
21	X509_V_ERR_UNABLE_TO_VERIFY_LE AF_SIGNATURE	no signatures could be verified because the chain contains only one certificate and it is not self signed.
22	X509_V_ERR_CERT_CHAIN_TOO_LONG	the certificate chain length is greater than the supplied maximum depth. Unused.
23	X509_V_ERR_CERT_REVOKED	the certificate has been revoked. Unused.
24	X509_V_ERR_INVALID_CA	a CA certificate is invalid. Either it is not a CA or its extensions are not consistent with the supplied purpose.
25	X509_V_ERR_PATH_LENGTH_EXCEEDE D	the basicConstraints pathlength parameter has been exceeded.
26	X509_V_ERR_INVALID_PURPOSE	the supplied certificate cannot be used for the specified purpose.
27	X509_V_ERR_CERT_UNTRUSTED	the root CA is not marked as trusted for the specified purpose.
28	X509_V_ERR_CERT_REJECTED	the root CA is marked to reject the specified purpose.
29	X509_V_ERR_SUBJECT_ISSUER_MISM ATCH	the current candidate issuer certificate was rejected because its subject name did not match the issuer name of the current certificate. Only displayed when the -issuer_checks option is set.
30	X509_V_ERR_AKID_SKID_MISMATCH	the current candidate issuer certificate was rejected because its subject key identifier was present and did not match the authority key identifier current certificate. Only displayed when

		the *issuer_checks* option is set.
3 1	X509_V_ERR_AKID_ISSUER_SERIAL_ MISMATCH	the current candidate issuer certificate was rejected because its issuer name and serial number was present and did not match the authority key identifier of the current certificate. Only displayed when the *issuer_checks* option is set.
3 2	X509_V_ERR_KEYUSAGE_NO_CERTSIG N	the current candidate issuer certificate was rejected because its keyUsage extension does not permit certificate signing.
5 0	X509_V_ERR_APPLICATION_VERIFIC ATION	an application specific error. Unused.

enc

The ENC utility will encrypt and decrypt files using the selected algorithm. The format is typically the following:

C:\>OpenSSL [ciphername] [options]
        Or
C:\>OpenSSL enc [ciphername] [options]

-in [filename]
This option sets the file to decrypt or encrypt.

-out [filename]
This option sets the output file.

-salt
This option will add a salt (random) value to the encryption. It is advised to use this option when encrypting files.

-e
Encrypt the specified data file. This is the default.

-d
Decrypt the specified data file

The following list represents the supported ciphers that can be used when encrypting or decrypting data.

Cipher	Description
base64	Base 64
bf-cbc	Blowfish in CBC mode
Bf	Alias for bf-cbc
bf-cfb	Blowfish in CFB mode
bf-ecb	Blowfish in ECB mode
bf-ofb	Blowfish in OFB mode
cast-cbc	CAST in CBC mode

Cast	Alias for cast-cbc
cast5-cbc	CAST5 in CBC mode
cast5-cfb	CAST5 in CFB mode
cast5-ecb	CAST5 in ECB mode
cast5-ofb	CAST5 in OFB mode
des-cbc	DES in CBC mode
des	Alias for des-cbc
des-cfb	DES in CBC mode
des-ofb	DES in OFB mode
des-ecb	DES in ECB mode
des-ede-cbc	Two key triple DES EDE in CBC mode
des-ede	Alias for des-ede
des-ede-cfb	Two key triple DES EDE in CFB mode
des-ede-ofb	Two key triple DES EDE in OFB mode
des-ede3-cbc	Three key triple DES EDE in CBC mode
des-ede3	Alias for des-ede3-cbc
des3	Alias for des-ede3-cbc
des-ede3-cfb	Three key triple DES EDE CFB mode
des-ede3-ofb	Three key triple DES EDE in OFB mode
desx	DESX algorithm.
idea-cbc	IDEA algorithm in CBC mode
idea	same as idea-cbc
idea-cfb	IDEA in CFB mode
idea-ecb	IDEA in ECB mode
idea-ofb	IDEA in OFB mode
rc2-cbc	128 bit RC2 in CBC mode
rc2	Alias for rc2-cbc
rc2-cfb	128 bit RC2 in CBC mode
rc2-ecb	128 bit RC2 in CBC mode
rc2-ofb	128 bit RC2 in CBC mode
rc2-64-cbc	64 bit RC2 in CBC mode
rc2-40-cbc	40 bit RC2 in CBC mode
rc4	128 bit RC4
rc4-64	64 bit RC4
rc4-40	40 bit RC4

rc5-cbc	RC5 cipher in CBC mode
rc5	Alias for rc5-cbc
rc5-cfb	RC5 cipher in CBC mode
rc5-ecb	RC5 cipher in CBC mode
rc5-ofb	RC5 cipher in CBC mode

In the above example we have chosen to encrypt a Word document using the rc4 cipher with a salt. The size of the file is the document you are reading and is approximately 22MB. This encryption only takes a few seconds to complete. The next example shows the decryption of the same file.

C:\>OpenSSL rc4 –d –in OpenDocEnc.doc –out OpenDocDec.doc

version
This utility will return the OpenSSL version being utilized.

-a
All information concerning the OpenSSL library.

PKCS12

This utility will create (PKCS#12) Personal Information Exchange (.pfx) files mostly used with Microsoft tools such as Internet Information Server. If you have ever gone through the process of getting an SSL certificate from Verisign or Thawte, then this is the certificate you will likely receive. You may therefore utilize the PKCS12 application to generate an SSL certificate for development purposes, remembering that the world according to most browsers will not accept your certificate unless it has been "signed" by one of the root certificates in your CA Trusted Roots list. To see the trusted roots in Windows go to Start | Run and type in "mmc" and press enter. This should bring up the Microsoft Management Console as seen in the next screen shot:

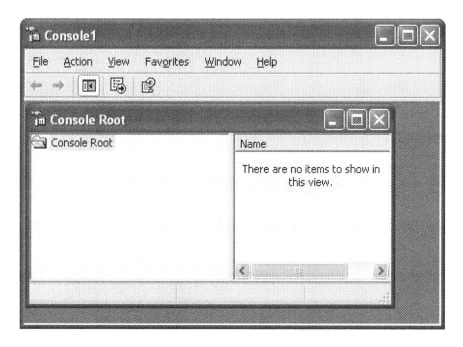

If you don't see exactly what is shown above, don't worry, screens will differ depending on the number of "snap-ins" you have loaded. To see the Trusted Root Certificates using the MMC select File | Add/Remove snap-in. The following dialog should appear:

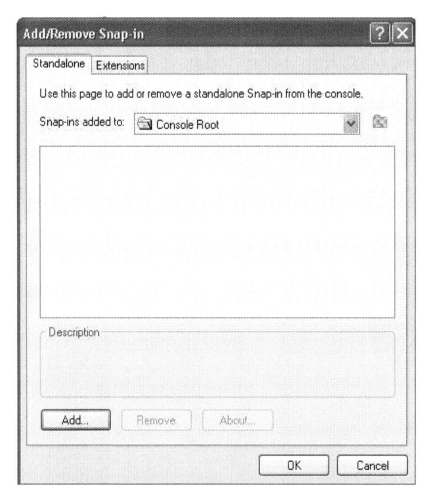

Press the Add… button in the bottom right corner to bring up the next dialog box as shown in the next screen shot:

From this dialog, navigate to the Certificates Snap and then press the Add button. You should now see the following dialog:

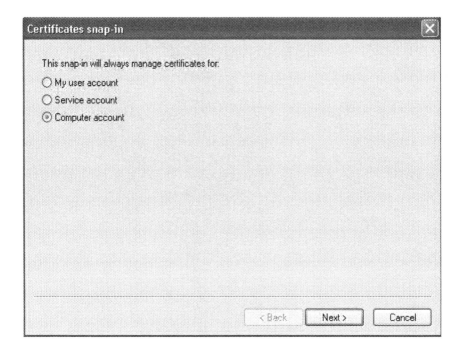

In the previous dialog make sure you select "Computer account" which will provide you all the certificates and lists for this computer, not just a user. Press the Next > button after making this selection. You should now see the following dialog:

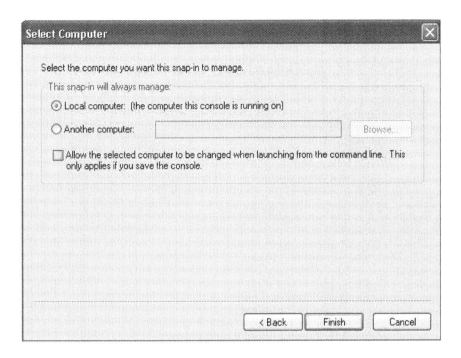

Make sure you select "Local computer: (the computer this console is running on)" and press the Finish button. This will take you to a prior screen at which point you should press the "Close" button or "Ok" button on all windows until you are back at the main Microsoft Management Console.

In the main MMC (Microsoft Management Console) you should now have the Certificates snap-in displayed in the left pane of the window. Your screen should now look something similar to the following. Pay close attention to the Trusted Root Certificate Authorities:

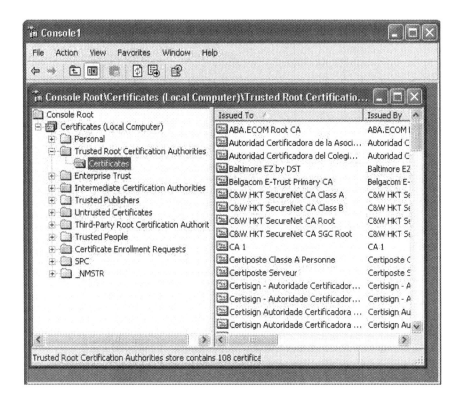

In the above right side pane notice that there are 108 certificates that this computer will trust. If you want to add your certificate to this list, right mouse click on the Certificates folder and select All Tasks | Import and go through the same process as shown earlier in section **Installing the CA Certificate into the Windows Operating System** making sure you are importing the proper format type of your certificate. For the PKCS#12 certificate format continue with this section.

Creating PKCS#12 Certificates in Internet Information Server

This part is the same process that will be utilized to create a Certificate Signing Request (CSR) that you would send to a

Certificate Authority such as Verisign or Thawte. To begin with you must make sure you Internet Information Server 5.0 which comes with Windows 2000 or XP. Windows NT4 users can usually follow the same steps but it may be slightly different. To begin with go to Start | Control Panel and double click on the Administrative Tools. In the Administrative Tools windows select Internet Information Services which will bring up the MMC with the IIS snap-in already loaded. Navigate to the Default Web Site in the left pane and right mouse click on the icon which should bring up the following pop up menu:

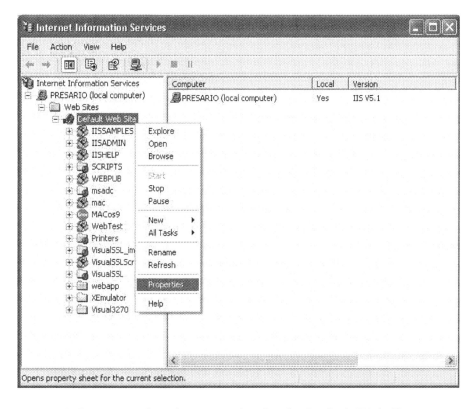

When you select the properties for the Default Web Site you should be presented with a tabbed dialog of the options for this site. Windows Workstations should note that they are limited to only the default web site whereas Windows Servers can have several web sites, of which one is usually an SSL enabled site utilizing a PKCS#12 certificate! Your screen, after selecting the Properties option, should look similar to the following:

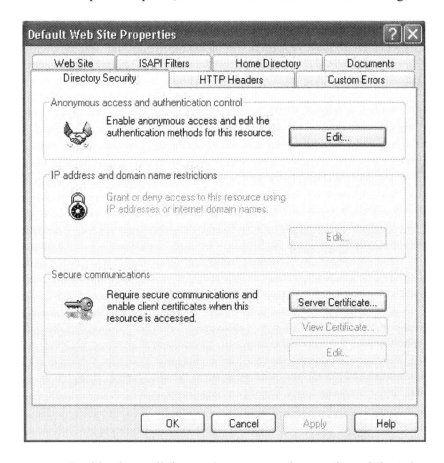

In this above dialog make sure you have selected the Directory Security tab and then the Server Certificate button. You should see the following dialog:

Press the Next > button on the previous screen shot if you have not already done so. You should see the next dialog. Select "Create a new certificate" and press the Next > button.

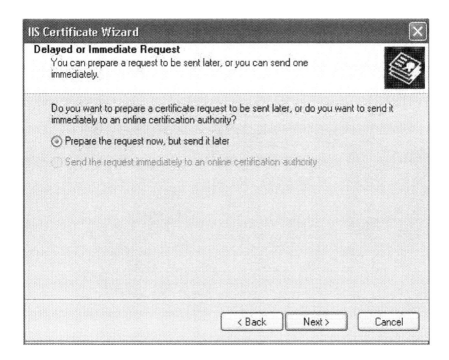

Select the "Prepare the request now, but send it later" option to create a Public Key pair and its associated Certificate Signing Request (CSR). You won't be able to view the key and public certificate immediately, but you will be able to view the CSR when you complete the whole process. We will discuss exporting the public key pair later in this section. If you have not already done so, press the Next > button:

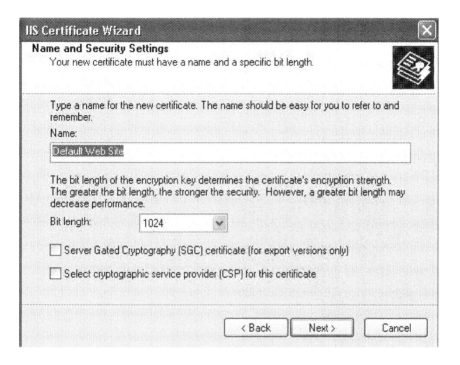

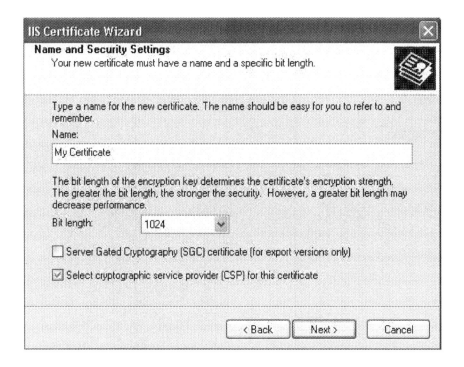

In the above dialogs select an easy to remember name with a bit length of 1024. If you have created a Public Key pair earlier using OpenSSL, this looks very familiar. Make sure you select the "Select cryptographic service provider (CSP) for this certificate." This will be important if using Authenticode and other technologies. After pressing the Next > button, make sure you select Microsoft RSA Schannel Cryptographic Provider and press the Next > button.

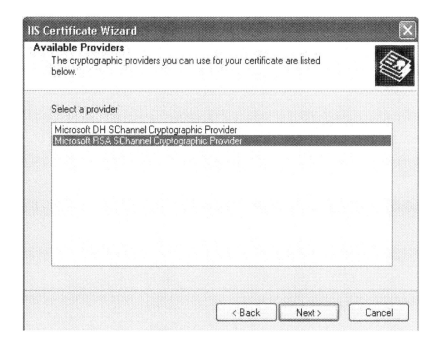

Schannel is Microsoft's answer to OpenSSL without the source code and open environment. This is commonly referred to as the CryptoAPI by Microsoft and is almost always found as a Dynamic Link Library.

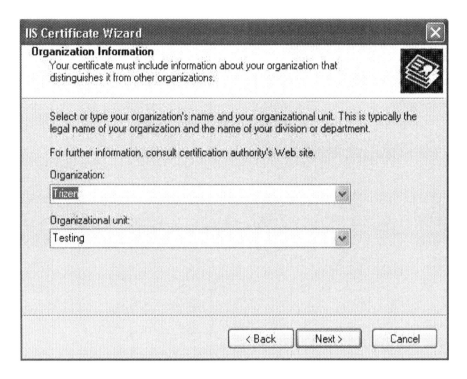

Add your information in the edit boxes provided in the above dialog. Don't worry if you make a mistake, you can always go back. Its only important when you are ready to send this information to a Certificate Authority.

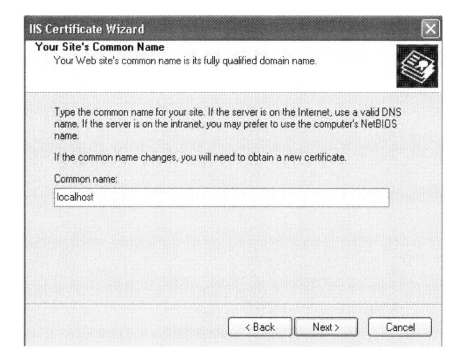

In the above dialog box place in your fully qualified domain name such as www.trizen.com or if you're only interested in testing, use localhost. Press the Next > button to complete the information regarding your certificate.

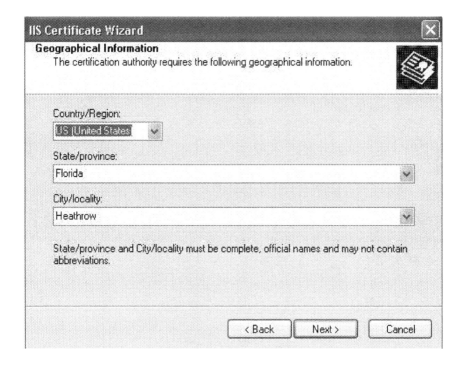

After filling in your information press the Next > button:

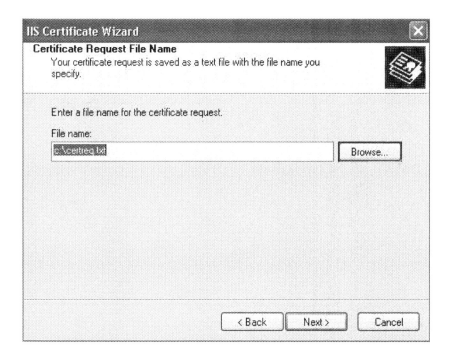

Select the filename and directory location where you would like to save your Certificate Signing Request. We typically save them near or in the CARoot directory created at the beginning of this document. When you press the Next > button you should see the following dialog:

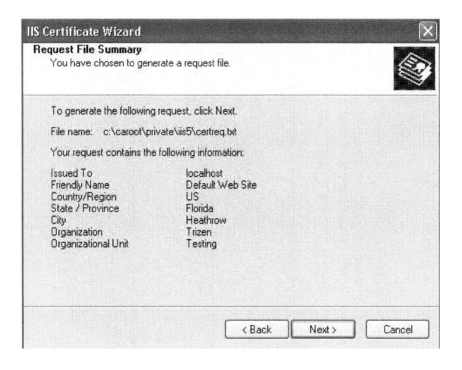

Press the Next > button to complete the certificate creation process.

Once you press the Finish button on the previous dialog, you should be taken back to the tabbed properties dialog for the Default Web Site. Press Cancel to return to the Internet Information Services Management Console. So where is the certificate and key file? It has been captured into the Microsoft Certificate's snap in. If you recall from the earlier discussion on locating all the Trusted Root Certificate Authorities by using the Certificates snap-in then you can easily export the certificate and key file from this utility as shown below:

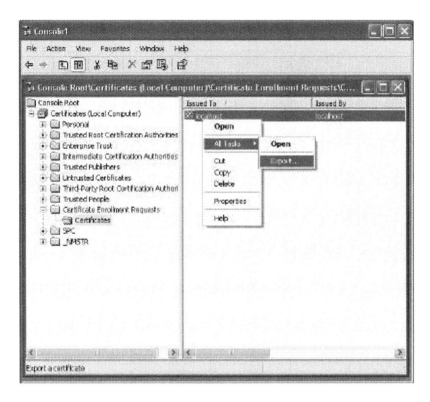

Notice that the certificate we just created is contained in the Certificate Enrollment Requests | Certificates files. Just right mouse click on the actual certificate in the right pane and select Export... to actually export the certificate.

Press the Next > button to continue the export process.

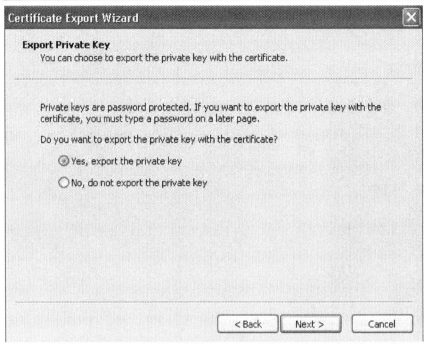

Make sure you select "Yes, export the private key" option.

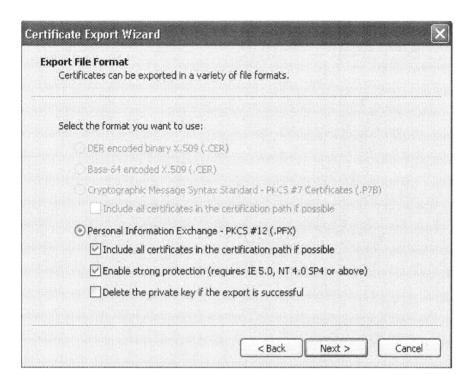

Make sure you select the same options as above.

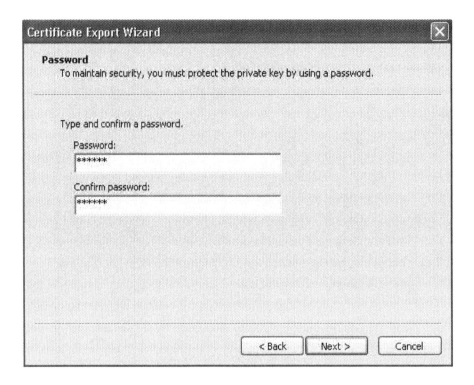

Type a password for your key file making sure you don't forget it!

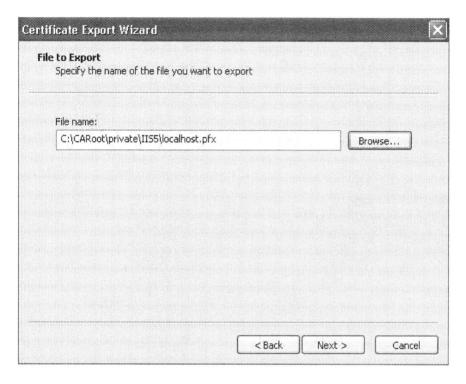

Select the filename for the key that will be exported as well as its location and press the Next > button. On the next screen just press Finish to complete the process.

At this point you have created a .pfx file that should reside in the directory you selected when you exported the file. We highly suggest you export these files near your CARoot directory structure. If you merely double click on the newly created .pfx file Windows will bring up the certificate import wizard, just press cancel if this pops up because what you really want is to look at the certificate and the key file. If you open the file up in WordPad you should see a lot of encrypted information:

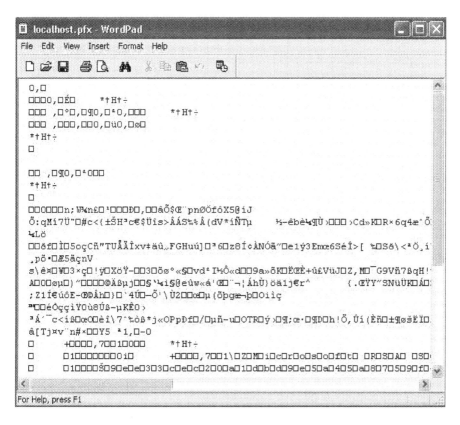

The above file is nowhere near human readable and as such needs to be parsed with the PKCS12 utility before the key and certificate can be viewed. If you have not already done so, create a directory named IIS5 in your c:\CARoot\private directory and place this .pfx file into this location. Next, open up the cmd.exe file or command.com file in your CARoot directory and type the following to parse your PKCS#12 certificate:

C:\CARoot>pkcs12 –in c:\CARoot\private\IIS5\localhost.pfx –out
c:\CARoot\private\IIS5\localhost.pem

You should notice that we are parsing the localhost.pfx file that
was exported earlier in this section. You may have a different
directory structure and as such your MS-DOS prompt may look
slightly different; however, the above demonstrates the parsing and
exporting of a new key and certificate file into one file. In our
demonstration we have copied the localhost.pfx file to the
c:\CARoot\private\IIS5 directory and exporting the parsed file to
the same location with the name localhost.pem. Notice that these
files are in PEM format. Before the file can be completely parsed
you must of course type in the password for the encrypted file that
was requested when you exported the localhost.pfx file. You
should keep this password when prompted to enter a password for

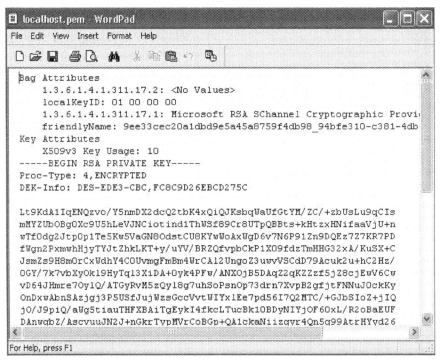

the localhost.pem file. At this point you can double click on the localhost.pem file:

This file should look somewhat familiar by now and can be used within your OpenSSL applications. OpenSSL applications allow the use of the certificate and the key within the same file as demonstrated by typing in the following into your MS-DOS prompt, assuming you have access to the OpenSSL applications via your PATH variable as discussed early during the install:

s_client −connect www.verisign.com:443 -ssl3 −cert
    c:\CARoot\private\IIS5\localhost.pem

Your screen should be very similar to the prior screen. If not, check your command and make sure you have access to the OpenSSL applications (the OpenSSL directory path is appended to your PATH environment variable) and the files you are point to in the command do in fact exist and you know the password. The interesting thing to do this time is to issue the following command when the connection is made:

GET / HTTP/1.0

This command is an HTTP request for the selected home page of the SSL host, in this case the Verisign home page should be returned after you press enter twice.

You should have received the home page of http://www.verisign.com after issuing the above command. HTTPS can be used with these and other commands to receive secure data from HTTPS servers. This is very convenient for communicating with e-commerce servers. For information on connecting to secure credit card companies you should consider purchasing Visual SSL at http://www.visualSSL.com.

If you would like to separate your key and certificate file you may do the following. First open the localhost.pem file and copy all the data of the certificate section.

```
-----BEGIN CERTIFICATE-----
MIIBzTCCAbqgAwIBAgIQJVgAkqbw4ptI23fbg50KkjAJBgUrDgMCHQUAMGkxEjAQ
BgNVBAMTCWxvY2FsaG9zdDEQMA4GA1UECxMHVGVzdGluZzEPMA0GA1UEChMGVHJp
emVuMREwDwYDVQQHEwhIZWF0aHJvdzEQMA4GA1UECBMHRmxvcmlkYTELMAkGA1UE
BhMCVVMwHhcNMDExMjExMDQxMDUzWhcNMDIxMjExMTAxMDUzWjBpMRIwEAYDVQQD
Ewlsb2NhbGhvc3QxEDAOBgNVBAsTB1Rlc3RpbmcxDzANBgNVBAoTBlRyaXplbjER
MA8GA1UEBxMISGVhdGhyb3cxEDAOBgNVBAgTB0Zsb3JpZGExCzAJBgNVBAYTAlVT
MIGfMA0GCSqGSIb3DQEBAQUAA4GNADCBiQKBgQCm9xkTPpcMmcNhDvpqpj9zLzPT
qJCL7Yb3qf27teXZxM5lphim8XZ80QxkdJ74UNT+WLapKHD+DXmZ/0UiDUQvO2oV
GLhyD9T3nhowwYXaK2/yegUCfpbpIDefy3AGGj/GbLiL5dIHofOX2DYg8xFOHIo+
EQKnat6RzRuCpo7LtQIDAQABMAkGBSsOAwIdBQADAgC+
-----END CERTIFICATE-----
```

Place the copied text into a new text file in your c:\CARoot\private\IIS5 directory and name it localhost.crt. Next, copy the private key data from the localhost.pem file:

```
-----BEGIN RSA PRIVATE KEY-----
Proc-Type: 4,ENCRYPTED
DEK-Info: DES-EDE3-CBC,FC8C9D26EBCD275C

Lt9KdA1IqENQzvo/Y5nmDX2dcQ2tbK4xQiQJKsbqWaUfGtYM/ZC/+zbUsLu9qCIs
mMYZUbOBg0Xc9U5hLeVJNCiotind1ThWSf89Cr8UTpQBBts+kHtzxHNifaaVjU+n
wTf0dg2Jtp0p1Te5Kw5VaGN8OdstCU8KYwWoAxWgD6v7N6P91Zn9DQEz7Z7KR7PD
fWgn2PxmwhHjyTYJtZhkLKT+y/uYV/BRZQfvpbCkP1X09fdzTmHHG32xA/KuSX+C
JsmZs9H8m0rCxWdhY4C0UvmgFmBm4WrCAl2UngoZ3uwvVSCdD79Acuk2u+hC2Hz/
0GY/7k7vbXyOkl9HyTql3XiDA+0yk4PFw/ANXOjB5DAqZ2qKZZzf5jZ8cjEwV6Cw
vD64JHmre7OylQ/ATGyRvM5zQyl8g7uhSoPsnOp73drn7XvpB2gfjtFNNuJ0ckKy
OnDxwAbnSAzjgj3P5USfJujWzsGccVvtWIYxlEe7pd56I7Q2MTC/+GJbSIoZ+jIQ
jO/J9piQ/aWg5tiauTHFXBAiTgEykI4fkcLTucBkl0BDyNIYjOF60xL/R2oBaEUF
DAnwqbZ/AscvuuJN2J+nGkrTypMVrCoBGp+QA1ckaNiizgyr4Qn5g99AtrHYyd26
bKhi/NcQFRLLPHYLnD8GG0nNQ3AYpt0MXS6e56LojqIRNN1/sG1wVl2IhDirfZQ1
21zBVx5f9WpWflQesFiBWMJshv7X9WMMvGoKNJNB4eDorf4qAPxEvdcp7/31M7rF
/u896eNQ//ipYAuEU8Ks88c5wyugQPBkcTCtyxudhvtgEddB0/1t0A==
-----END RSA PRIVATE KEY-----
```

Place the copied data into a new text file in your c:\CARoot\private\IIS5 directory and name it localhost.key. You now have two separated files and they each can be used within OpenSSL applications. Remember though that you have separated your public certificate and private key file and as such you must specify both for any OpenSSL applications that require a certificate and key file.

We have digressed from the original format slightly to demonstrate some of the ways OpenSSL can be utilized in Windows operating systems. At this point we will demonstrate the more utilized options with the PKCS12 utility.

-in [filename]
Use this option to set the PKCS#12 certificate to be processed. The following command will parse the localhost.pfx and place its private key and public certificate into out.pem.

C:\CARoot>pkcs12 – in localhost.pfx –out out.pem

-out [filename]
Use this option to specify the output file that will hold the key and certificate in one file.

C:\CARoot>pkcs12 – in c:\CARoot\private\IIS5\localhost.pfx –out out.pem

-nokeys
Use this option to output only a certificate. You will only be prompted for a password to the PKCS#12 file (if encrypted with a password). If you want to use the newly created certificate in windows you must remove the extra header information from the – out file after it is created.

C:\CARoot>pkcs12 – in localhost.pfx –nokeys –out out.pem

-info
This options really only add a little information about the process that is taking place with the command.

C:\CARoot>pkcs12 – in localhost.pfx – info –out out.pem

-des, -des3, -idea
Use one of these options to specify the encryption algorithm to protect the key.

C:\CARoot>pkcs12 – in localhost.pfx –des3 –out.pem

-nodes

Use this option to NOT encrypt the keys. This means the keys will not be password protected for use. Not recommended.

    C:\CARoot>pkcs12 –in localhost.pfx –nodes –out.pem

-noout

Select this option to keep the utility from creating any output. Usually used with –info switch. The following example demonstrates the use of sending information about a certificate contained in the directory c:\CARoot\private\IIS to the screen.

    C:\CARoot>pkcs12 –in private\IIS\localhost.pfx –noout –info

-password [pass:password]

Use this option when specifying a password that must be used to access a file when creating a PKCS#12 file. This format will have the password displayed on the command line. For example, if your password was visualssl then the format would be:

    C:\CARoot>pkcs12 –export –in localhost.pem –out mypkcs12.pfx
                   –password pass:visualssl

-inkey [filename]

If using this option then the –in file will usually be just a certificate. If both the certificate and key file are in the same file, then just use –in file.

    C:\CARoot>pkcs12 –export –in private\temp.crt –inkey
    private\temp.key –out
                   mypkcs12.pfx

-export

Use this option to CREATE a PKCS#12 file. You must supply at least one private key and one certificate usually in one file. This next example will take a .pfx file and parse it into a .pem file which will have the key and certificate contained within it encrypted.

C:\CARoot>pkcs12 – in localhost.pfx –out localhost.pem

The next line will then take this localhost.pem file and turn it back into a PKCS#12 file using the password that was used:

C:\CARoot>pkcs12 –export –in localhost.pem –out mypkcs12.pfx
–password pass:mypass

At this point the file can be double clicked on in Microsoft Windows and imported into a Trusted Certificate Store. The next example shows how to use an already created certificate file and a key file to generate a PKCS12 file.

Step 1) Generate a Key File

C:\CARoot>*genrsa –out private\temp.key –rand private\.rnd –des3 2048*

Step 2) Generate a Certificate File from the above key

C:\CARoot>*req –new –x509 –days 3650 –key private\temp.key – out private\temp.crt –config openssl.cnf*

Step 3) Copy the Certificate File data into the temp.key file

As you can see from the above screen shot we have pasted the temp.crt information (by opening temp.crt in WordPad) into the temp.key file. Make sure there are no lines between the dashed lines and no extra lines at the bottom.

Step 4) Save the file as combined.pem

Step 5) Create the PKCS#12 file

```
C:\CARoot>pkcs12 -export -in private\combined.pem -out
mypkcs12.pfx
Loading 'screen' into random state - done
Enter PEM pass phrase:
Enter Export Password:
Verifying password - Enter Export Password:

C:\CARoot>
```

From the above MS-DOS command prompt screen shot we have issued the following command:

C:\CARoot>pkcs12 –export –in private\combined.pem –out mypkcs12.pfx

If you now double click on the new mypkcs12.pfx file in the C:\CARoot directory you will be prompted by windows to import the file. You can just press Cancel if you wish or go ahead and import the file. If you did not get the desired results make sure you have followed the instructions carefully realizing that creating key files and certificates were covered in great detail early in this manual and are sometimes very tricky.

Ok, here is an easier way if you don't want to copy text from one file to another by simply using the generated Certificate temp.crt and the Key file temp.key.

Step 1) Generate a Key File

C:\CARoot>*genrsa –out private\temp.key –rand private\.rnd –des3 2048*

Step 2) Generate a Certificate File from the above key

C:\CARoot>*req –new –x509 –days 3650 –key private\temp.key – out private\temp.crt –config openssl.cnf*

Step 3) Create a PKCS#12 File from the temp.key and temp.crt

The command is virtually the same as before except we are explicitly telling the PKCS utility that there is a separate key file through the use of the –inkey switch. The utility would then expect the –in file to be just a certificate:

C:\CARoot>pkcs12 –export –in private\temp.crt –inkey private\temp.key –out mypkcs12.pfx

Authenticode and Digitally Signing Your Applications

For those that are interested in learning how to create ActiveX controls and have them operate from within Internet Explorer even when the security is High, then you should sign your ActiveX controls and applications with an Authenticode Certificate which is nothing more than a PKCS#12 signed certificate.

The process is relatively straight forward and summarized as follows:

1) Create a Certificate Request from Internet Information Server (described in PKCS#12 section)
2) Sign the Certificate as follows:

   C:\CARoot>ca –in private\IIS5\certreq.txt –key private\ca.key – out private\IIS\trizen.cer –policy policy_anything –config openssl.cnf

3) Complete the Internet Information Server certificate process by returning to the same place in IIS to create the certificate request. Import the newly signed certificate.
4) Use Microsoft Management Console to export the certificate as a PKCS#12 certificate to c:\CARoot\private\IIS5\trizen.pfx
5) Parse the newly created trizen.pfx file using the PKCS12 utility:

   C:\CARoot>pkcs12 –in private\IIS5\trizen.pfx –out private\IIS5\trizen.pem

6) Separate the key portion from the newly created trizen.pem file making it compatible to Windows (removing everything but the ----BEGIN RSA PRIVATE KEY ---- and ---- END RSA PRIVATE KEY -----.
7) Save the newly created key file to c:\CARoot\private\IIS5\trizen.key

8) Create a PKCS#12 certificate file using the signed certificate trizen.crt and the exported key file trizen.key using the following command:

C:\CARoot\>pkcs12 –export –in private\IIS5\trizen.cer –inkey
    private\IIS5\trizen.key –out private\IIS5\newtrizen.pfx

9) Double-click on the newtrizen.pfx file and import it into windows.
10) Download the Authenticode SDK from Microsoft.com and run the signcode.exe application.
11) Select your ActiveX control or .cab file to sign and use the certificate store. It should have the newly imported PKCS#12 certificate.
12) Complete the code signing process, realizing that you should let Microsoft select the Security Provider which should be captured already in the operating system during the import.

Did you get all that? If not here is the process in more excruciating detail. Remember, if you're interested in learning about Authenticode, you should review the Microsoft technologies of Cabinet files, and ActiveX distribution. For more information on ActiveX distribution, safe code, digitally signed code, you should consider purchasing our VisualSSL product.

Complete Detail of Creating Authenticode Applications

Create a Certificate Request using the methods described in the **Creating PKCS#12 Certificates in Internet Information Server** section. Make sure you save this file in c:\CARoot\private\IIS5\certreq.txt.

Sign the certificate request using the following command:

C:\CARoot>ca –in private\IIS5\certreq.txt –key private\ca.key –config
    openssl.cnf –policy policy_anything –out private\IIS5\trizen.cer

You must make sure that you have setup your Certificate Authority structure and that your paths are accurate including your PATH environment variable which must include the directory to the OpenSSL applications.

Once the certificate has been signed, you must make sure that you modify the certificate to conform to the Windows Operating System. See Adjusting the Certificates for Windows Operating Systems for more information.

At this point you must return to the Internet Information Server security area and complete the Certificate Request Process. Return to the same location where you first initiated the Certificate Request. Upon returning to this dialog you should see the following:

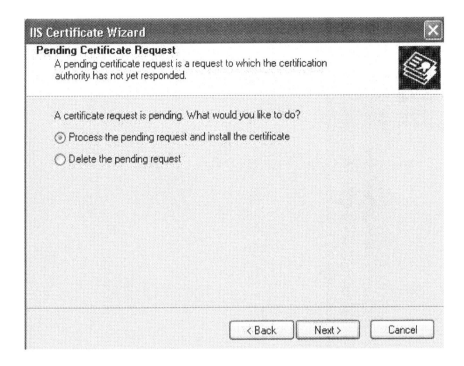

Notice that IIS is waiting for the signed certificate that was created earlier. At this point press the Next > button and navigate to the trizen.crt file.

At this point press the Next > button.

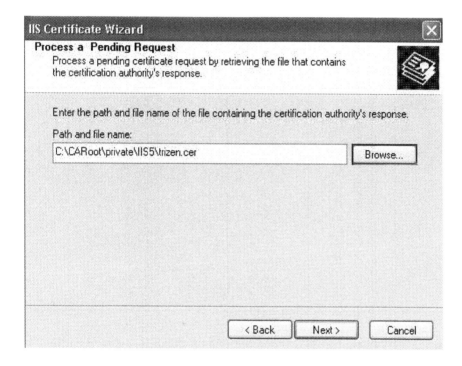

If you do not see the above dialog after pressing the Next > button review your certificate by double clicking on it making sure Windows recognizes the certificate. After pressing the Next > button you will likely get the following:

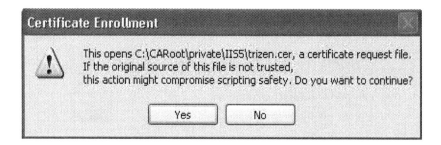

Just press Yes to continue. Windows will notify you that the process is complete. You may have noticed that at this point you are performing the same actions to create an SSL server. In fact press the Edit button in the secure communications area of the Directory Security Tab of the Default Web Site properties. You should see the following dialog which will allow you to make your server SSL enabled:

If you select the "Require secure channel (SSL)" and press OK, your server will only accept secure connections! To see this in action after you press the OK button, open up Internet Explorer and type in https://127.0.0.1 and you should see your default web page, but this

time the secure connection icon can be found in your web browser's status bar. You must realize that since Internet browsers have a limited list of trusted certificates, others may not be able to connect to your site because their browsers do not know of your certificate, they will likely be prompted to continue loading the page.

Now back to Authenticode. After you have completed the CSR process by first creating a certificate request, signing the request, and then importing the signed certificate into IIS, you must now export the key and certificate as a PKCS#12 file. This is the same process as described in the PKCS12 Utility application and will not be repeated here, however, when you export the PKCS#12 certificate, make sure you export it to c:\CARoot\private\IIS5\trizen.pfx. The store that it will likely be in will be in the Local Computer account in the Personal store, you may have to search to find your certificate, looking for the certificate property such as http://www.trizen.com which is usually the common name of the server.

After you successfully exported the Key and Certificates (by right mouse clicking on the certificate and selecting export) into a PKCS#12 file (trizen.pfx) you must now parse the file so that you can have an independent key file by first issuing the following command:

C:\CARoot>pkcs12 –in private\IIS5\trizen.pfx –out private\IIS5\trizen.pem

The above command will export the key associated with the certificate that was created along with the certificate request. We had to export it in this format to get it out of the Windows operating system. Your file should look similar to:

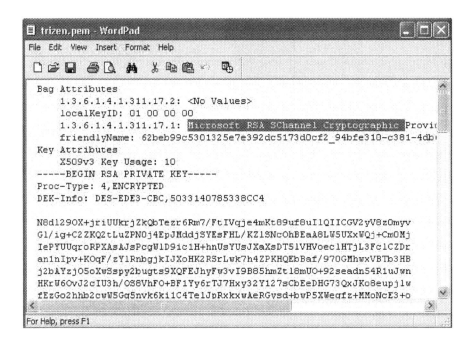

Notice that in the above file the property of Microsoft RSA Schannel Cryptographic Provider. This can only be accomplished by creating a certificate from within IIS and selecting this option during the creation phase.

At this point you must separate the private key from the rest of the file by following the similar approach to separating certificates manually from the extraneous information. Your key should look like the following:

```
-----BEGIN RSA PRIVATE KEY-----
Proc-Type: 4,ENCRYPTED
DEK-Info: DES-EDE3-CBC,5033140785338CC4

N8dl29OX+jriUUkrjZkQbTezr6Rm7/FtIVqje4mKt89uf8uIlQIICGV2yV8z0myv
Gl/ig+C2ZKQ2tLuZPN0j4EpJMddjSYEsFHL/KZlSNcOhBEaA8LW5UXxWQj+CmOMj
IePYUUqroRPXAsAJsPcgWlD9ic1H+hnUsYUsJXaXsDT5lVHVoeclHTjL3FclCZDr
an1nIpv+KOqF/zYlRnbgjkIJXoHK2RSrLwk7h4ZPKHQEbBaf/970GMhwxVBTb3HB
j2bAYzjO5oXwSspy2bugts9XQFEJhyFw3vI9B85hmZtl8mUO+92seadn54R1uJwn
HKrW6OvJ2cIU3h/OS8VhFO+BF1Yy6rTJ7Hxy32Y127sCbEeDHG73QxJKo8eupjlw
fEzGo2hhb2cwW5Gg5nvk6ki1C4TelJpRxkxwAeRGysd+bwP5XWegfz+MMoNcE3+o
3a90E0Qi/vjp/fkbrjpwn62DSIwEypi7CkStFfrGxkWsV7HPkQUrnZWFCptEOw8b
0qoI1D3EslvC3a/e4XotrpVnQQAiE+Ljln7/IN6k+/96TxKTGeFK/RnCRsiPwTvr
rNEzbrWtS2guxFhDWrJHoNBJM8qW3sp+Gd1MW4L2jTEMSZO0pjCtU9wsGt2uPh+v
YU2Y2iBwlDCbDFlM17yqZdniVduExrR80HkmEBi4gzp8FmUwNu8J2Gm/bhEi5D8n
H+GXTVaagcEx2HfofdwM5PoXwLocugIGK1Xjxo9wZA9OxqYoUDmE64+PMMhFmFJF
SMCWUZixmtxTB8obRr5fcePSzgOYJTHnejqPD/pHC9U=
-----END RSA PRIVATE KEY-----
```

Save this key information to c:\CARoot\private\IIS5\trizen.key. We now have several files that will be utilized:

File	Description
Certreq.txt	Our IIS Certificate Request
Trizen.cer	The Signed Certificate by our CA
Trizen.key	The Exported key of the Certificate Request. From Trizen.pem
Trizen.pfx	The Exported PKCS#12
Trizen.pem	The Parsed file of the PKCS#12 file. Certificate and Key.

We must now build a PKCS#12 file which will be imported into Windows. Type the following command to create a new PKCS#12 certificate:

C:\CARoot>pkcs12 –export –in private\IIS5\trizen.cer –inkey private\IIS5\trizen.key
    -out private\IIS5\NewTrizen.pfx

129

This PKCS#12 file must now be imported into windows. Simply double click on the newly created NewTrizen.pfx file. Windows will prompt you to begin the Certificate Import Wizard. Just continue until you get to the following dialog:

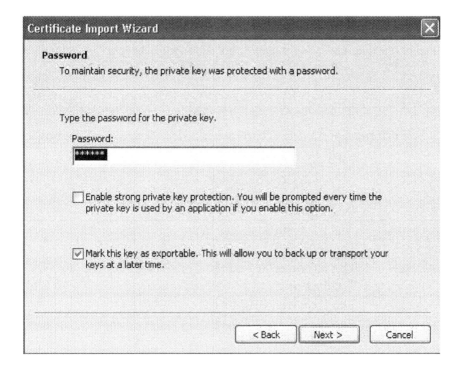

Type in the password for your private key, this was set when you issued your certificate request. Also, check the "Mark this key as exportable. This will allow you to back up or transport your keys at a later time."

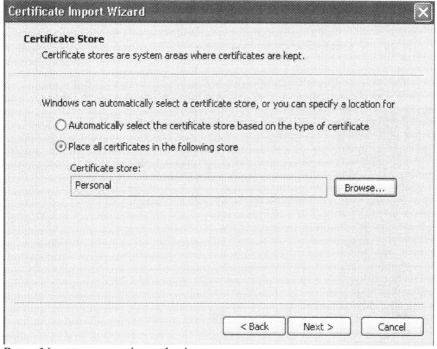

Press Next > to continue the import process:
Make sure you place the certificate into the Personal Store by browsing for its location. Press Next > to continue the process. The next dialog will finish the process. Just press Finish, or Ok to complete the import.

You now have all the items you need to successfully add a digital signature to your applications. At this point you should have already created your ActiveX controls and either packed them into a Microsoft Cabinet file or left them as an .ocx ready for distribution over the internet. In order to completely utilize your application in Internet Explorer without those irritating dialogs, you must mark your application as "safe" using and you must use Authenticode. Both of which still don't guarantee safety, but do give your customers a better feeling.

If you have not already done so, download Microsoft's Authenticode SDK at http://msdn.microsoft.com/downloads/ where you should look for Authenticode. Download your version. Once you have the SDK installed you need to run the signcode.exe application only after you have built your ActiveX control or Cabinet file. For information on building a successful Internet Explorer ActiveX control, you should purchase VisualSSL for information.

Press the Next > button to continue the Digital Signature process.

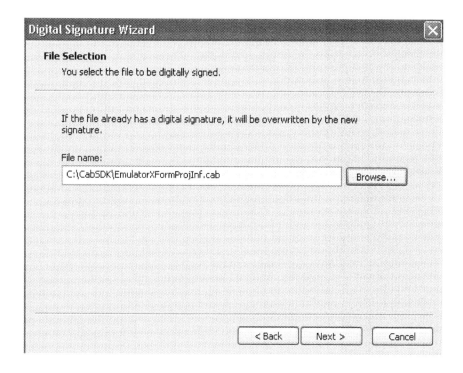

In this dialog, locate your ActiveX control (.ocx) or in the example's case, your Microsoft Cabinet file. This is the application you are signing. Many times you will have to sign multiple cabinet files. Press Next > to continue:

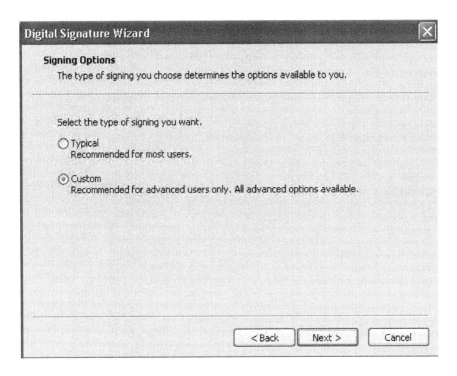

Since our certificate is already contained in our Personal Certificate store, choosing either the Typical or Custom option will have the same result; however, for those that are importing a file, you must use the Custom option. After pressing the Next > button you should press the "Select from Store" button (this will be the only option if you selected Typical).

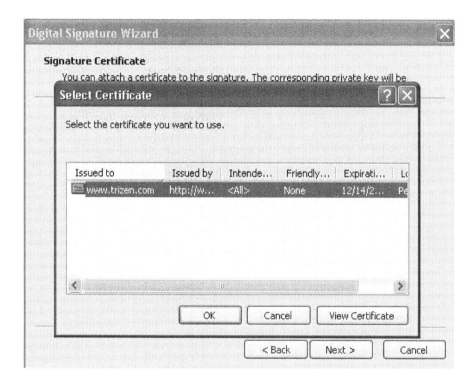

If all has gone well you should see the PKCS#12 certificate imported earlier. Select this certificate by pressing the OK button. If you did not see this in your dialog, make sure you have followed the directions exactly as outlined. Press Next > to continue the code signing process.

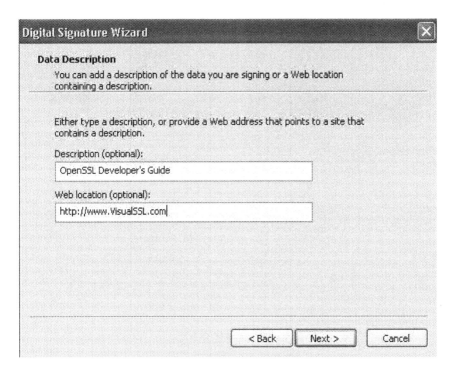

When your Authenticode certificate is presented to the end user, the information that you type into the above dialog will also be presented with a hypertext link to your site. Press Next > to continue.

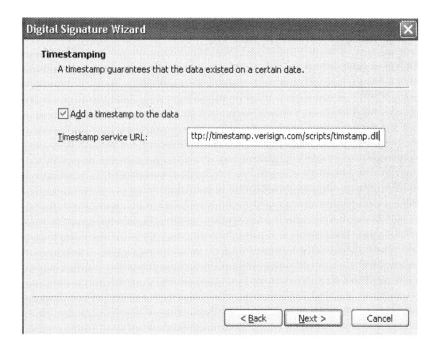

The timestamp dialog offers you an opportunity to timestamp your certificates to differentiate them if necessary and discourage forgeries. This is completely optional and if desired type the following into the edit box:

http://timestamp.verisign.com/scripts/timstamp.dll

After pressing the Next > button you will be presented with the following dialog which will complete the code signing process:

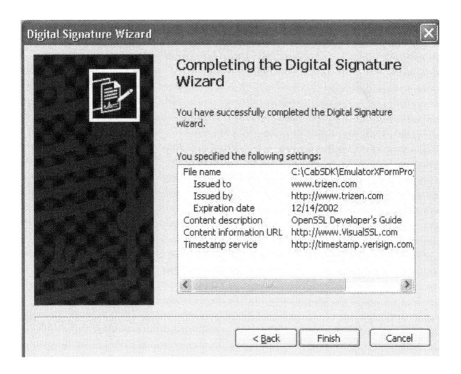

Press the Finish button to complete the process. Your code has now been Digitally signed by your Certificate Authority. Remember this is not the only step to make your controls simple for download use when Internet Explorer's security settings are high. For an in depth look at creating ActiveX controls for use over the Internet check out our website at http://www.trizen.com.

OpenSSL and Delphi

Using the OpenSSL library within Delphi offers great simplicity. Many people and programmers have believed that there has to be a Delphi "header" file full of prototypes based upon the OpenSSL library—This is completely unnecessary as Delphi makes using the OpenSSL library very, very easy. In this section we will demonstrate the use of the OpenSSL library for use from within Delphi.

First and foremost when using OpenSSL from within Delphi, it is best and easiest to use the SSL libraries as dynamically loaded libraries. These libraries will add an extra 400K to your applications, but makes it very easy to add SSL to socket applications. The two libraries are:

    Libeay32.dll
    SSLeay32.dll

It's not necessary to fully understand what each library does, but it may be worth while reviewing the OpenSSL source code to get a better understanding of these libraries and their functions. Currently there are around 3,000 functions in these libraries as seen from Microsoft Visual C++ def files for libeay32 and ssleay32 projects.

All that is necessary is to make sure that these libraries are accessible to your Delphi application. This can be by way of the system32 directory or other path variable or by adding them directly to your application directory.

So lets get started. The first thing to do is to realize that even though we don't have to recreate the prototypes for all the different type of structures, pointers, and other variables, we must actually make use of a converted prototype list for all the important SSL functions needed. The following pages represent a unit that you should create to make use of the SSL functions:

Just add this unit to any Delphi project's uses clause and you're ready to go.

```
//////////////////////////////////////////////////////////////////////////////
//
//  TinyWeb Copyright (C) 1997-2000 RIT Research Labs
//
//  This programs is free for commercial and non-commercial use as long as
//  the following conditions are aheared to.
//
//  Copyright remains RIT Research Labs, and as such any Copyright notices
//  in the code are not to be removed. If this package is used in a
//  product, RIT Research Labs should be given attribution as the RIT Research
//  Labs of the parts of the library used. This can be in the form of a textual
//  message at program startup or in documentation (online or textual)
//  provided with the package.
//
//  Redistribution and use in source and binary forms, with or without
//  modification, are permitted provided that the following conditions are
//  met:
//
//  1. Redistributions of source code must retain the copyright
//     notice, this list of conditions and the following disclaimer.
//  2. Redistributions in binary form must reproduce the above copyright
//     notice, this list of conditions and the following disclaimer in the
//     documentation and/or other materials provided with the distribution.
//  3. All advertising materials mentioning features or use of this software
//     must display the following acknowledgement:
//     "Based on TinyWeb Server by RIT Research Labs."
//
//  THIS SOFTWARE IS PROVIDED BY RIT RESEARCH LABS "AS IS" AND ANY EXPRESS
//  OR IMPLIED WARRANTIES, INCLUDING, BUT NOT LIMITED TO, THE IMPLIED
//  WARRANTIES OF MERCHANTABILITY AND FITNESS FOR A PARTICULAR PURPOSE ARE
//  DISCLAIMED. IN NO EVENT SHALL THE AUTHOR OR CONTRIBUTORS BE LIABLE FOR
//  ANY DIRECT, INDIRECT, INCIDENTAL, SPECIAL, EXEMPLARY, OR CONSEQUENTIAL
//  DAMAGES (INCLUDING, BUT NOT LIMITED TO, PROCUREMENT OF SUBSTITUTE
//  GOODS OR SERVICES; LOSS OF USE, DATA, OR PROFITS; OR BUSINESS
//  INTERRUPTION) HOWEVER CAUSED AND ON ANY THEORY OF LIABILITY, WHETHER
//  IN CONTRACT, STRICT LIABILITY, OR TORT (INCLUDING NEGLIGENCE OR
//  OTHERWISE) ARISING IN ANY WAY OUT OF THE USE OF THIS SOFTWARE, EVEN IF
//  ADVISED OF THE POSSIBILITY OF SUCH DAMAGE.
//
//  The licence and distribution terms for any publically available
//  version or derivative of this code cannot be changed. i.e. this code
//  cannot simply be copied and put under another distribution licence
//  (including the GNU Public Licence).
//
//////////////////////////////////////////////////////////////////////////////

unit SSLeayServerv_fp;

interface uses Windows;


type
```

```
  PCharArray = ^TCharArray;
  TCharArray = array[0..MaxLongInt-1] of Char;
type
  //added of object everywhere
  TTmpRsaCallbackFunc = function(P: Pointer; I, J: Integer): Pointer of object;
register;
  TVerifyCallbackFunc = function(ok: Integer; ctx: Pointer): BOOL of object; regi
  TLockingCallbackProc = procedure(Amode: integer; Atype: integer; Afile: PChar;
integer); cdecl;
  TMallocFunc = function(Size: Integer): Pointer; cdecl;
  TReallocFunc = function (Block: Pointer; Size: Integer): Pointer; cdecl;
  TFreeProc = procedure (Block: Pointer); cdecl;
  Tpem_passwd_cb = function (buf: Pointer; size: integer; rwflag: integer;
                        userdata: Pointer): integer of object; cdecl;

const
  X509_V_OK              = 0;
  X509_FILETYPE_PEM      = 1;
  X509_FILETYPE_ASN1     = 2;
  X509_FILETYPE_DEFAULT      = 3;
  NID_commonName         = 13;

  SSL_FILETYPE_ASN1      = X509_FILETYPE_ASN1;
  SSL_FILETYPE_PEM       = X509_FILETYPE_PEM;

  RSA_3                  = $3;
  RSA_F4                 = $10001;

// use either SSL_VERIFY_NONE or SSL_VERIFY_PEER, the last 2 options
// are 'ored' with SSL_VERIFY_PEER if they are desired
  SSL_VERIFY_NONE                 = $00;
  SSL_VERIFY_PEER                 = $01;
  SSL_VERIFY_FAIL_IF_NO_PEER_CERT = $02;
  SSL_VERIFY_CLIENT_ONCE          = $04;

  SSL_SENT_SHUTDOWN     = 1;
  SSL_RECEIVED_SHUTDOWN = 2;
  SSL_CTRL_OPTIONS      = 32;
  BIO_C_SET_CONNECT     = 100;
  BIO_C_GET_FD          = 105;
  BIO_C_SET_NBIO        = 102;
  BIO_C_SET_SSL             = 109;
  BIO_CLOSE             = $01;
  BIO_NOCLOSE           = $00;

  CRYPTO_NUM_LOCKS      = 24;

  CRYPTO_LOCK           = 1;
  CRYPTO_UNLOCK             = 2;
  CRYPTO_READ           = 4;
  CRYPTO_WRITE          = 8;



  //X509 ERROR MESSAGES FOR VERIFY
  X509_V_ERR_CERT_CHAIN_TOO_LONG      = 22;
```

```
procedure  CRYPTO_set_locking_callback(cb: TLockingCallbackProc); cdecl;
procedure  CRYPTO_set_mem_functions(malloc_func: TMallocFunc; realloc_func:
TReallocFunc; free_func: TFreeProc); cdecl;
function   EVP_PKEY_copy_parameters(Ato, Afrom: Pointer): Boolean; cdecl;
function   RAND_load_file(FName: PChar; Sz: Integer): Integer; cdecl;
function   RSA_generate_key(bits: Integer; e: Integer; cb, cba: Pointer): Pointe
cdecl;
function   SSL_CTX_check_private_key(ctx: Pointer): BOOL; cdecl;
function   SSL_CTX_new(meth: Pointer): Pointer; cdecl;
procedure  SSL_CTX_set_verify(ctx: Pointer; Mode: Integer; cb: TVerifyCallbackFu
cdecl;
procedure  SSL_set_verify(ssl: Pointer; Mode: Integer; cb: TVerifyCallbackFunc)
function   SSL_CTX_set_tmp_rsa_callback(ctx: Pointer; cb: TTmpRsaCallbackFunc):
cdecl;
function   SSL_CTX_use_certificate_file(ctx: Pointer; FName: PChar; AType: Intec
Integer; cdecl;
function   SSL_use_certificate(ssl: Pointer; x: Pointer): integer; cdecl;
function   SSL_use_certificate_file(ssl: Pointer; FName: PChar; AType: integer)
integer; cdecl;
function   SSL_CTX_use_PrivateKey_file(ctx: Pointer; FName: PChar; AType: Intege
Integer; cdecl;
function   SSL_CTX_load_verify_locations(cts: Pointer; CAFile: PChar; CAPath: Pe
integer; cdecl;
function   SSL_accept(ssl: Pointer): Integer; cdecl;
procedure  SSL_free(ssl: Pointer); cdecl;
function   SSL_get_certificate(ssl: Pointer): Pointer; cdecl;
function   SSL_get_privatekey(ssl: Pointer): Pointer; cdecl;
procedure  SSL_library_init; cdecl;
procedure  SSL_load_error_strings; cdecl;
function   SSL_new(ctx: Pointer): Pointer; cdecl;
function   SSL_read(ssl: Pointer; var Buf; num: Integer): Integer; cdecl;
function   SSL_peek(ssl: Pointer; var buf; num: integer): integer; cdecl;
function   SSL_set_fd(ssl: Pointer; fd: Integer): integer; cdecl;
procedure  SSL_set_shutdown(ssl: Pointer; Mode: Integer); cdecl;
function   SSL_write(ssl: Pointer; const Buf; num: Integer): Integer; cdecl;
function   SSLv23_server_method: Pointer; cdecl;
function   SSLv3_server_method: Pointer; cdecl;
function   TLSv1_server_method: Pointer; cdecl;
function   TLSv1_client_method: Pointer; cdecl;
function   X509_get_pubkey(x: Pointer): Pointer; cdecl;
procedure  SSL_set_accept_state(s: Pointer); cdecl;
function   SSLv3_client_method: Pointer; cdecl;
function   SSLv23_client_method: Pointer; cdecl;
procedure  OpenSSL_add_all_algorithms; cdecl;
function   SSL_CTX_set_cipher_list(ctx: Pointer; str: PChar): integer; cdecl;
procedure  ERR_load_crypto_strings; cdecl;
function   BIO_new(typ: Pointer): Pointer; cdecl;
function   BIO_s_connect: Pointer;  cdecl;
function   BIO_ctrl(bp: Pointer; cmd: integer; larg: longint; parg: PChar): Lonc
cdecl;
procedure  SSL_set_connect_state(ssl: Pointer); cdecl;
procedure   SSL_set_bio(s: Pointer; rbio: Pointer; wbio: Pointer); cdecl;
function   SSL_connect(ssl: Pointer): integer; cdecl;

//Authentication and Verify Callback functions
```

```
function X509_STORE_CTX_get_current_cert(ctx: Pointer): Pointer; cdecl;
function X509_STORE_CTX_get_error(ctx: Pointer): integer; cdecl;
function X509_STORE_CTX_get_error_depth(ctx: Pointer): integer; cdecl;
function SSL_get_peer_certificate(ssl: Pointer): Pointer; cdecl;
function SSL_get_verify_result(ssl: Pointer): integer; cdecl;
procedure SSL_CTX_set_verify_depth(ctx: Pointer; depth: integer); cdecl;
procedure SSL_set_verify_depth(ssl: Pointer; depth: integer); cdecl;
function X509_NAME_oneline(a: Pointer; buf: array of char; size: Integer): Pointer;
cdecl; //cast to character string
function X509_get_subject_name(a: Pointer): Pointer; cdecl;
function X509_get_issuer_name(a: Pointer): Pointer; cdecl;
procedure X509_STORE_CTX_set_error(ctx: Pointer; s: integer); cdecl;
procedure SSL_CTX_set_default_passwd_cb(ctx: Pointer; PasswordCallbackFunc:
Tpem_passwd_cb); cdecl;
function X509_NAME_get_text_by_NID(name: Pointer; nid: integer; buf: PChar; len:
integer): integer; cdecl;
procedure SSL_CTX_set_default_passwd_cb_userdata(ctx: Pointer; u: PChar);  cdecl;
function ERR_error_string(e: integer; buf: PChar): PChar; cdecl;
function ERR_get_error: integer; cdecl;



implementation

const
  ssldll   = 'ssleay32.dll';
  libdll   = 'libeay32.dll';


procedure  CRYPTO_set_locking_callback(cb: TLockingCallbackProc); cdecl; external
libdll;
procedure  CRYPTO_set_mem_functions(malloc_func: TMallocFunc; realloc_func:
TReallocFunc; free_func: TFreeProc); cdecl; external libdll;
function   EVP_PKEY_copy_parameters(Ato, Afrom: Pointer): Boolean; cdecl; external
libdll;
function   RAND_load_file(FName: PChar; Sz: Integer): Integer; cdecl; external lib
function   RSA_generate_key(bits: Integer; e: Integer; cb, cba: Pointer): Pointer
cdecl; external libdll;
function   SSL_CTX_check_private_key(ctx: Pointer): BOOL; cdecl; external ssldll;
function   SSL_CTX_new(meth: Pointer): Pointer; cdecl; external ssldll;
function   SSL_CTX_set_tmp_rsa_callback(ctx: Pointer; cb: TTmpRsaCallbackFunc): Po
cdecl; external ssldll
procedure  SSL_CTX_set_verify(ctx: Pointer; Mode: Integer; cb: TVerifyCallbackFunc
cdecl; external ssldll;
procedure  SSL_set_verify(ssl: Pointer; Mode: Integer; cb: TVerifyCallbackFunc); c
external ssldll;
function   SSL_CTX_use_PrivateKey_file(ctx: Pointer; FName: PChar; AType: Integer)
Integer; cdecl; external ssldll;
function   SSL_CTX_use_certificate_file(ctx: Pointer; FName: PChar; AType: Integer
Integer; cdecl; external ssldll;
function   SSL_use_certificate(ssl: Pointer; x: Pointer): integer; cdecl; external
ssldll;
function   SSL_use_certificate_file(ssl: Pointer; FName: PChar; AType: integer):
integer; cdecl; external ssldll;
function   SSL_CTX_load_verify_locations(cts: Pointer; CAFile: PChar; CAPath: PCha
integer; cdecl; external ssldll;
```

```
function   SSL_accept(ssl: Pointer): Integer; cdecl; external ssldll;
procedure  SSL_free(ssl: Pointer); cdecl; external ssldll;
function   SSL_get_certificate(ssl: Pointer): Pointer; cdecl; external ssldll;
function   SSL_get_privatekey(ssl: Pointer): Pointer; cdecl; external ssldll;
procedure  SSL_library_init; cdecl; external ssldll;
procedure  SSL_load_error_strings; cdecl; external ssldll;
function   SSL_new(ctx: Pointer): Pointer; cdecl; external ssldll;
function   SSL_read(ssl: Pointer; var Buf; num: Integer): Integer; cdecl; exter
ssldll;
function   SSL_peek(ssl: Pointer; var buf; num: integer): integer; cdecl; exter
ssldll;
function   SSL_set_fd(ssl: Pointer; fd: Integer): integer; cdecl; external ssld
procedure  SSL_set_shutdown(ssl: Pointer; Mode: Integer); cdecl; external ssldl
function   SSL_write(ssl: Pointer; const Buf; num: Integer): Integer; cdecl; ex
ssldll;
function   SSLv23_server_method: Pointer; cdecl; external ssldll;
function   SSLv3_server_method: Pointer; cdecl; external ssldll;
function   TLSv1_server_method: Pointer; cdecl; external ssldll;
function   TLSv1_client_method: Pointer; cdecl; external ssldll;
function   X509_get_pubkey(x: Pointer): Pointer; cdecl; external libdll;
procedure  SSL_set_accept_state(s: Pointer); cdecl; external ssldll;
function   SSLv3_client_method: Pointer; cdecl; external ssldll;
function   SSLv23_client_method: Pointer; cdecl; external ssldll;
procedure  OpenSSL_add_all_algorithms; cdecl; external libdll;
function   SSL_CTX_set_cipher_list(ctx: Pointer; str: PChar): integer; cdecl; e
ssldll;
procedure  ERR_load_crypto_strings; cdecl; external libdll;
function   BIO_new(typ: Pointer): Pointer; cdecl; external libdll;
function   BIO_s_connect: Pointer;  cdecl; external libdll;
function   BIO_ctrl(bp: Pointer; cmd: integer; larg: longint; parg: PChar): Lon
cdecl; external libdll; //see next line
procedure  SSL_set_connect_state(ssl: Pointer); cdecl; external ssldll;
procedure   SSL_set_bio(s: Pointer; rbio: Pointer; wbio: Pointer); cdecl; exter
ssldll;
function   SSL_connect(ssl: Pointer): integer; cdecl; external ssldll;

//Authentication and Verification Callback functions
function X509_STORE_CTX_get_current_cert(ctx: Pointer): Pointer; external libdl
function X509_STORE_CTX_get_error(ctx: Pointer): integer; external libdll;
function X509_STORE_CTX_get_error_depth(ctx: Pointer): integer; external libdll
function SSL_get_peer_certificate(ssl: Pointer): Pointer; external ssldll;
function SSL_get_verify_result(ssl: Pointer): integer; external ssldll;
procedure SSL_CTX_set_verify_depth(ctx: Pointer; depth: integer); cdecl; extern
ssldll;
procedure SSL_set_verify_depth(ssl: Pointer; depth: integer); external ssldll;
function X509_NAME_oneline(a: Pointer; buf: array of char; size: Integer): Poin
external libdll; //cast to character string
function X509_get_subject_name(a: Pointer): Pointer; external libdll;
function X509_get_issuer_name(a: Pointer): Pointer; external libdll;
procedure X509_STORE_CTX_set_error(ctx: Pointer; s: integer); external libdll;
procedure SSL_CTX_set_default_passwd_cb(ctx: Pointer; PasswordCallBackFunc:
Tpem_passwd_cb); cdecl; external ssldll;
function X509_NAME_get_text_by_NID(name: Pointer; nid: integer; buf: PChar; len
integer): integer; external libdll;
procedure SSL_CTX_set_default_passwd_cb_userdata(ctx: Pointer; u: PChar);  cdec
external ssldll;
function ERR_error_string(e: integer; buf: PChar): PChar; cdecl; external libdl
```

```
function ERR_get_error: integer; cdecl; external libdll;

end.
```

In the preceding sample code it should be paid special attention to how the pointers are used as generic pointer structures when matching the OpenSSL libraries. This is the best part about Delphi, you don't have to prototype the exact struct, or pointer to make use of the SSL libraries, just call it a Pointer and the computer will figure out the rest. For instance the following is the exact prototype for one of the SSL functions as written in C++:

```
typedef struct ssl_st SSL;
int   SSL_connect(SSL *ssl);
```

In the above code you will find that ssl_st is a huge structure of such complexity that it would be very difficult to actually import the prototype into Delphi. For this reason, Delphi provided the Pointer type so that this was easy to overcome. In other words, if you didn't want to go through and convert the ssl_st struction, you could simply use the Delphi prototype as follows:

```
function   SSL_connect(ssl: Pointer): integer; cdecl;
```

Notice that the above Delphi prototype makes no use of specific structures like SSL or ssl_st, and replaces these complex structures with the keyword Pointer. Easy and to the point, so if you have reason to create a prototype based on another function not in the above Delphi prototype list, just make your own using the Pointer keyword and save yourself a lot of time.

Now that we have added our SSL "prototypes" it is time to create our component. In the following source code snippet we have created a component that will make use of windows messages, bw level sockets, and SSL libraries that will be encapsulated in the Visual SSL component library. If you have never created a component in Delphi, don't sweat it, just take out the code you want and put it into your application. Pay particular attention to SetSSL3 which pretty much is the SSL portion of the code.

```
//////////////////////////////////////////////////////////////////////
//
//   SSLClientSocket version 1.0
//   Trizen Systems Incorporated
//
//   This is an Asynchronous Event model Non-Blocking client TCP/IP Socket.
//   There is on other model: A blocking socket; however we will not
//   be using this in this component.  This model is best for continuous
//   connection sockets that are not serial.
//
//   Ths example uses SSL as the read and write methods from the OpenSSL
//   organization. http://www.openssl.org.  The library files must
//   be present in a directory that is a part of the path variable, it
//   is recommended to place these files (ssleay32.dll, libeay32.dll)
//   in the winnt (for NT 4+), windows (winMe -) or system32 directories;
//   however if using multiple applications that access this, you may
//   consider placing these files within the application directory.
//
//   For more information contact:
//
//       Trizen Systems, Inc. http://www.trizen.com
//       407.417.4164
//
//   NOTE:  In order to send certificates, you must send the key file
//          as well as the cert file!
//
//   NOTE:  There is no "Server authentication" with respect to a
//          key store of certificates to trust.  This client socket
//          will supply a call back to the developer OnCertReceived()
//          that will send along the certificate, along with it
//          comes a reference variable of ErrorOut, and is up to
//          the developer to either set it to TRUE or FALSE.
//
//
//
//   NOTE:  DEVELOPERS MUST MAKE SURE THEY READ UNTIL NO DATA IS AVAILABLE
//          i.e. Length of string or return data is 0 (-1) during an OnRead
//          event or make sure they read the maximum number of bytes
//          possible
//          that a server could send!  See HTTPS examnple connecting
//          to https://secure.rtware.net
//
//   12-18-01 Removed SSL_CTX_set_default_passwd_cb. Replaced with
//            SSL_CTX_set_default_password_cb_userdata.
//              Allows different passwords.
//
//   12-18-01 Added cmSSLv23 to ConnectMethod.  see meth.
//   2-10-02 Removed if Connected from FD_READ.
//
//////////////////////////////////////////////////////////////////////


{$ifdef VER100}
    {$define DELPHI3}
{$endif}
{$ifdef VER120}
    {$define DELPHI4}
```

147

```
{$endif}
{$ifdef VER130}
    {$define DELPHI5}
{$endif}
{$ifdef VER140}
    {$define DELPHI6}
{$endif}

unit SSLClientSocket;

interface

uses
  Windows, Messages, SysUtils, Classes, Graphics, Controls, Forms,
Dialogs,
  SSLeayServerv_fp, Winsock, WinProcs, extctrls{$ifdef
DEMO},DemoExpiration {$endif};


const
WM_ASYNCHRONOUSPROCESS = WM_USER + 101; //EZ Message number for
asynchronous socket messages}
WM_WAITFORRESPONSE = WM_USER + 102;      //EZ custom message number for
synchronous responses
MAX_RECV_BUF = 65000;
FD_ALL = 63;   //Short for FD_READ or FD_WRITE.... in the WSAAsyncSelect
Statement!!
CR = #13;
LF = #10;
CRLF = #13#10;

 //Socket Error Event
type
  ESSLSocketError = class(Exception);
  TOnSSLError = procedure (Sender: TObject; Code: integer; ErrorMsg:
String) of object;
  TOnWndProc = procedure (Sender: TObject; var Msg: TMessage) of object;
  TOnCertReceived = procedure (Sender: TObject; ssl: Pointer; X509Cert:
Pointer; Issuer: String;
                              peerCN: String; var ErrorOut: boolean) of
Object;
  TOnPasswordRequired = procedure(Sender: TObject; var ErrorOut: boolean)
of object;

type
  TConnectMethod = (cmSSLv23, cmSSLv3, cmTLSv1);
//The Property Page aka Property Editor, this is a string


type
  TSSLClientSocket = class(TComponent)
  private
    FCipherList: String;
    FOnSSLError: TOnSSLError;
    FHandleErrors: boolean;
    FOnDestroy: TNotifyEvent;
```

```
    FOnCreate: TNotifyEvent;
    FSocketHandle: HWND;
    FProxy: String;
    FHost: String;
    FPort: integer;
    FProxyPort: integer;
    FTimeout: integer;
    FOnHostResolved: TNotifyEvent;
    FOnConnect: TNotifyEvent;
    FOnDisconnect: TNotifyEvent;
    FOnRead: TNotifyEvent;
    FOnWrite: TNotifyEvent;
    FCertLocation: String;
    FRandLocation: String;
    FOnWndProc: TOnWndProc;
    FKeyLocation: String;
    FOnCertReceived: TOnCertReceived;
    FConnectMethod: TConnectMethod;
    SockAvailable: boolean;  //global variable for determining if Winsock
is available or not!! See Initialize
    FKeyPassword: String; //will assign the GlobalKeyPassword variable.

    FOnPasswordRequired: TOnPasswordRequired;
    FCanceled: boolean;


    procedure xSSLeayInit;
    function SetSSL3: boolean;
    procedure ThrowError(E: integer);
    procedure TimerFired(Sender: TObject);
  protected
    RemoteAddress: TSockAddr; //Address of remote host}
    RemoteHost: PHostEnt; //Entity to store remote host linfo from a
Hostname request
    ThreadTimer: TTimer; //The timeout Timer!
    ResolveError: boolean;
    ConnectError: boolean;
    DestroySocket: boolean;
    Succeed: boolean;
    Timedout: boolean;
    PasswordRequested: boolean;

    procedure RequestCloseSocket;
    procedure Wndproc(var Msg: TMessage);
    function GetLocalIP: string;
    function GetRemoteIP: string;


  public
    ssl_ctx: Pointer;   //BIO Context Underlying SSL
    meth: Pointer;      //We are only dealing with meth = SSLv3
    servercon: Pointer; //The SSL Connection
    ThisSocket: TSocket; //The infamous socket!!
    Connected: boolean;
    MyWSAData: TWSAData; //  Right from the Winsock.pas! the ^TWSAData
packed record!!
```

```
constructor Create(AOwner: TComponent); override;
destructor Destroy; override;
procedure Connect;
procedure ClearInput;
function ReadBuf(var Buf: array of char; sizebuf: integer): integer;
function Read: String;
function Write(Buf: String; sizebuf: integer): integer;
function WriteBuf(Buf: array of char; sizebuf: integer): integer;
procedure Disconnect;

property Canceled: boolean read FCanceled write FCanceled;
property SocketHandle: HWND read FSocketHandle;
property LocalIP: string read GetLocalIP;
property RemoteIP: string read GetRemoteIP;

function ProcWnd: boolean; //12-10-01


published

property HandleErrors: boolean read FHandleErrors write FHandleErrors;
property CipherList: String read FCipherList write FCipherList;
property OnSSLError: TOnSSLError read FOnSSLError write FOnSSLError;
property OnDestroy: TNotifyEvent read FOnDestroy write FOnDestroy;
property OnCreate: TNotifyEvent read FOnCreate write FOnCreate;
property Host: String read FHost write FHost;
property Port: integer read FPort write FPort;
property Timeout: integer read FTimeout write FTimeout;
property OnHostResolved: TNotifyEvent read FOnHostResolved write
FOnHostResolved;
property OnConnect: TNotifyEvent read FOnConnect write FOnConnect;
property OnDisconnect: TNotifyEvent read FOnDisconnect write
FOnDisconnect;
property OnRead: TNotifyEvent read FOnRead write FOnRead;
property OnWrite: TNotifyEvent read FOnWrite write FOnWrite;
property OnWndProc: TOnWndProc read FOnWndProc write FOnWndProc;
property CertLocation: String read FCertLocation write FCertLocation;
property RandLocation: String read FRandLocation write FRandLocation;
property KeyLocation: String read FKeyLocation write FKeyLocation;
property OnCertReceived: TOnCertReceived read FOnCertReceived write
FOnCertReceived;
property ConnectMethod: TConnectMethod read FConnectMethod write
FConnectMethod;
property KeyPassword: String read FKeyPassword write FKeyPassword;
property OnPasswordRequired: TOnPasswordRequired read
FOnPasswordRequired write FOnPasswordRequired;

default 3000;

end;


function SSLClientSocketAllocateHwnd(Obj: TObject): HWND;

implementation
```

```
constructor TSSLClientSocket.Create(AOwner: TComponent);
var
v: String;
begin
    inherited Create(AOwner);
    //Create a Handle!
    FSocketHandle :=  SSLClientSocketAllocateHwnd(self);
    FCipherList := 'EXP-RC4-MD5';
    FHandleErrors := true;
    Connected := false;
    Canceled := false;
    DestroySocket := false;
    SockAvailable := WSAStartUp($0101, MyWSADATA) <> -1;
    FConnectMethod := cmSSLv3;
    if not(csDesigning in ComponentState) then
     begin
      GetMem(RemoteHost, MAXGETHOSTSTRUCT); //Nasty error if you leave this
out!
      ThreadTimer := TTimer.Create(self);
      ThreadTimer.Enabled := false;
      ThreadTimer.Interval := FTimeout;
      ThreadTimer.OnTimer := TimerFired;

{$ifdef DEMO}
{$ifdef DELPHI3}
     v := '3.0';
{$endif}
{$ifdef DELPHI4}
     v := '4.0';
{$endif}
{$ifdef DELPHI5}
     v := '5.0';
{$endif}
{$ifdef DELPHI6}
     v := '6.0';
{$endif}

    if (not CheckRegistry(v)) then
     begin
       MessageBox(0, 'Visual SSL 1.0 Demonstration.  License is expired.',
'Trizen Demo', MB_OK);
     end;

{$endif}
    end;

   if Assigned(FOnCreate) then
     FOnCreate(self);
end;//--

destructor TSSLClientSocket.Destroy;
begin
 try
```

```
  DestroySocket := True;


  if SockAvailable then WSACleanUp;
  if not(csDesigning in ComponentState) then
    begin
      FreeMem(RemoteHost, MAXGETHOSTSTRUCT);
      ThreadTimer.Destroy;
      RequestCloseSocket;
    end;
  if (servercon <> nil) then
    begin
      SSL_set_shutdown(servercon, SSL_SENT_SHUTDOWN or
SSL_RECEIVED_SHUTDOWN);
      SSL_free(servercon);
    end;
  if (FSocketHandle > 0) then
    DestroyWindow(FSocketHandle); //very important

 except
 end;
 if Assigned(FOnDestroy) then
    FOnDestroy(self);
 inherited Destroy;
end;//-------------------------------------------------------------------
----

procedure TSSLClientSocket.xSSLeayInit;
begin

  SSL_library_init;
  SSL_load_error_strings;

end;//-------------------------------------------------------------------
----

//Dispatcher for ISAPI Application Object.
function TSSLClientSocket.ProcWnd: boolean;
var
Handled: Boolean;
Msg: TMsg;
i: integer;

begin

        if PeekMessage(Msg,0,0,0,PM_REMOVE) then  //Check the Messages!
          begin
            Result := true;
            if Msg.Message <> WM_QUIT then
             begin
               Handled:= false;
               TranslateMessage(Msg); //No VK Messages
               DispatchMessage(Msg);
             end;
          end
        else
         Application.ProcessMessages;
```

```
end;

function TSSLClientSocket.SetSSL3: boolean;
var
ch: array[0..3000] of char;
ret: integer;
i: integer;
fd_width: integer;
conn: Pointer;
//SSLAttempts: integer;
temp_ssl, x509: Pointer;
peer: Pointer; //x509 server certificate
buf: array[0..400] of char; //hold server certificate data
SubjectStr: String;
peer_CN: array[0..255] of char;
peerCN: String;
StopProcessing: boolean;

errorbuf: array[0..255] of char;
errorout: boolean;
begin

  ZeroMemory(@errorbuf, 255);
  ZeroMemory(@ch, 3000);
  result := false;
  xSSLeayInit;
  if (FConnectMethod = cmSSLv3) then
    meth := SSLv3_client_method
  else
    if (FConnectMethod = cmTLSv1) then
      meth := TLSv1_client_method
    else
      meth := SSLv23_client_method;

  OpenSSL_add_all_algorithms;
  RAND_load_file(PChar(FRandLocation), $100000);
  ssl_ctx := SSL_CTX_new(meth);
  if (SSL_CTX_set_cipher_list(ssl_ctx, PChar(FCipherList)) <= 0) then
    begin
      ThrowError(2);
      exit;

    end;


  //SSL_CTX_set_default_passwd_cb(ssl_ctx, FOnClientPassword);
  SSL_CTX_set_default_passwd_cb_userdata(ssl_ctx, PChar(FKeyPassword));

  if (FCertLocation <> '') then  //The client is providing a Public and
Private Key!
    begin


      if (SSL_CTX_use_certificate_file(ssl_ctx, PChar(FCertLocation),
SSL_FILETYPE_PEM) <= 0) then
        begin
```

153

```
          ThrowError(3);
          exit;
        end;


     if ( SSL_CTX_use_PrivateKey_file(ssl_ctx, PChar(FKeyLocation),
SSL_FILETYPE_PEM) <= 0) then
        begin
            //SSL_CTX_set_default_passwd_cb_userdata(ssl_ctx,
PChar(FKeyPassword));

            i := ERR_get_error; //get last error code
            ERR_error_string(i, errorbuf);  //Translate to human readable
format


            if (i = 151429224) or (i=101077092) then   //KeyPassword is
not accurate or missing
              begin
                repeat
                 errorout := true;
                 if Assigned(FOnPasswordRequired) then
                   FOnPasswordRequired(self, errorout);

                 SSL_CTX_set_default_passwd_cb_userdata(ssl_ctx,
PChar(FKeyPassword));
                 if (SSL_CTX_use_PrivateKey_file(ssl_ctx,
PChar(FKeyLocation), SSL_FILETYPE_PEM) <= 0) then
                   begin
                     if (errorout) then
                      begin
                        ThrowError(25);
                        exit;
                       end;
                   end
                   else
                     break; //password is ok!! Whoo Whoo!
                  until false;
                end
              else
               begin
                 ThrowError(4);
                 exit;
                end;
          end;
       temp_ssl := SSL_new(ssl_ctx);

       x509 := SSL_get_certificate(temp_ssl);

       if x509 <> nil then EVP_PKEY_copy_parameters(X509_get_pubkey(x509),
SSL_get_privatekey(temp_ssl));

       SSL_free(temp_ssl);

       if not SSL_CTX_check_private_key(ssl_ctx) then
         begin
```

154

```
          ThrowError(5);
          exit;
        end;

    end;


    ERR_load_crypto_strings;

    conn := BIO_new(BIO_s_connect);
    if conn = nil then
     begin
      ThrowError(8);
      exit
     end;
    ret := BIO_ctrl(conn,BIO_C_SET_NBIO,1,''); //Make the underlying BIO a
non-blocking socket!
    if (ret <= 0) then
       begin
        ThrowError(9);
        exit;
       end;

       servercon := SSL_new(ssl_ctx);
       SSL_set_connect_state(serverCon);
       SSL_set_bio(servercon, conn, conn);
       fd_width := SSL_set_fd(servercon, ThisSocket) + 1;
       Timedout := false;
       ThreadTimer.Enabled := true;


       repeat
         i := SSL_connect(servercon);
         if (i > 0) then
          Connected := true;
         Application.ProcessMessages;
       until (i > 0) {or (SSLAttempts > FSSLAttempts)} or (Canceled) or
(Timedout); //roughly 10 seconds worth of attempts
       ThreadTimer.Enabled := false;

       if (Canceled) then
        begin
           ThrowError(14);
           exit;
        end;
       if (Timedout) then
        begin
          ThrowError(19);
          exit;
        end;

    //Check the server's certificate!
    peer := SSL_get_peer_certificate(servercon);
    if (peer <> nil) then
      begin

        //Add a user event here
```

```
        X509_NAME_oneline(X509_get_subject_name(peer),buf,400);
        SubjectStr := buf;
        ZeroMemory(@buf, 200);
        X509_NAME_oneline(X509_get_issuer_name(peer),buf,400);
        SubjectStr := buf;
        X509_NAME_get_text_by_NID(X509_get_subject_name(peer),
NID_commonName, peer_CN, 256);
        peerCN := peer_CN;
        StopProcessing := false;
        if Assigned(FOnCertReceived) then
           FOnCertReceived(self, servercon, peer, SubjectStr,
peerCN,StopProcessing);
        if (StopProcessing) then
          begin
           closesocket(ThisSocket);
           exit
          end;


     end;

   result := true;


end;
procedure WaitforSync(Handle: THandle; interval: integer);

begin
  repeat
    if MsgWaitForMultipleObjects(1, Handle, False, interval, QS_ALLINPUT)
= WAIT_OBJECT_0 + 1 then
       begin
         Application.ProcessMessages;
         if interval <> -1 then break;
       end
    else
       BREAK;
  until True = False;
end;


procedure TSSLClientSocket.ThrowError(E: integer);
var
S: String;

begin
  case E of
    1:   S := 'Socket Error: Closed unexpectedly on read.';
    2:   S := 'SSL Error: Could not load the SSL encryption.';
    3:   S := 'SSL Error: The Application could not load the specified
Public Certificate.';
    4:   S := 'SSL Error: The Application could not load the specified Key
file.';
    5:   S := 'SSL Error: The Public Certificate and Key File do not
match';
    6:   S := 'SSL Error: Set verify paths returned false';
```

```
   7:   S := 'SSL Error: Set verify locations returned false';
   8:   S := 'SSL Error: The BIO cannot be created.';
   9:   S := 'SSL Error: The BIO cannot be created in non-blocking socket
(Async) mode.';
   10:  S := 'SSL Error: The Application was unnable to connect in SSL
Mode.  Too many attempts.';
   11:  S := 'SSL Error: The Socket was shut down.  No SSL Server or bad
address.';
   12:  S := 'Socket Error: Already Connected.';
   13:  S := 'Socket Error: Socket timedout on resolving host.';
   14:  S := 'Socket Error: Canceled by user.';
   15:  S := 'Socket Error: Socket could not resolve host.';
   16:  S := 'Socket Error: Invalid socket descriptor.';
   17:  S := 'Socket Error: Error on WSAAyncSelect.';
   18:  S := 'Socket Error: Error on connection; WSAGetLastError.';
   19:  S := 'Socket Error: Timedout on connection.';
   20:  S := 'Socket Error: Could not connect to host.';
   21:  S := 'Winsock Error: incorrect winsock version, must be 1.1 or
higher.';
   22:  S := 'Winsock Error: No address available.';
   23:  S := 'Error on Read.';
   24:  S := 'Error on Write.';
   25:  S := 'SSL Error: Private Key Password Incorrect.';


  else
    S := 'Socket Error: General error.';

  end; //end case

  //Handle user defined events and other items!
  if Assigned(FOnSSLError) then
    FOnSSLError(self, E, S);
  if (FHandleErrors) then
   begin
     raise ESSLSocketError.Create(S);
   end;
end; //------------------------------------------------------------------
------

procedure TSSLClientSocket.WndProc(var Msg: TMessage);
begin


    if Assigned(FOnWndProc) then
      FOnWndProc(self, Msg);
    with Msg do
      begin


        case Msg of

          WM_ASYNCHRONOUSPROCESS:
           begin

             if LParamHi > 0 then
```

157

```
      ConnectError := True
   else
      Succeed := True;
   case LParamLo of

     FD_CONNECT:
       if Succeed then
         begin

           if (not SetSSL3) then //Must initialize all SSL
Connections, must have client.pem in directory
             begin
              Disconnect;
              exit;
             end;

           if Assigned(FOnConnect) then
             FOnConnect(self);
         end;

     FD_CLOSE:
       begin
         try
           if Connected then
             begin
               //ClearInput;
               Connected := FALSE;

             end;
           RequestCloseSocket;
         except
         end;
         if assigned(FOnDisconnect) then
             FOnDisconnect(self);
       end;

     FD_READ:
         begin

           //if (Connected) then
             if assigned(FOnRead) then
               FOnRead(self);
         end;
     FD_WRITE:
         begin
           if assigned(FOnWrite) then
             FOnWrite(self);
         end;
   end; //end case of lParamLo
 end; //End WM_ASYNCHRONOUSPROCESS:
WM_WAITFORRESPONSE:
     begin
       if LParamHi > 0 {SOCKET_ERROR} then
         ResolveError := True
       else
         Succeed := True;
```

```
                    end;
          end;
        end;
   //inherited WndProc(Msg); //standard inherit from TComponent at
beginning
end; //---------------------------------------------------------------
------


procedure TSSLClientSocket.Connect;
var
  I: Integer;
  Handled: Boolean;
  HostBuf: array[0..100] of char;
begin

    PasswordRequested := false;
    ThreadTimer.Interval := FTimeout;   //Set here
    if not SockAvailable then
     begin
      ThrowError(21);
      exit;
     end;

    Canceled := False;
    if Connected then //already connected, throw an error
     begin
       ThrowError(12);
       exit;
     end;
    if (ThisSocket > 0) then
      ThisSocket := 0;

    ThisSocket := Socket(PF_INET, SOCK_STREAM, IPPROTO_TCP);
    if ThisSocket = SOCKET_ERROR then
     begin
      ThrowError(16);
      exit;
     end;
    WSAAsyncselect(ThisSocket, FSocketHandle, WM_ASYNCHRONOUSPROCESS,
FD_ALL);

    if FProxy = '' then
       RemoteAddress.sin_addr.S_addr := Inet_Addr(StrPCopy(HostBuf,
FHost))
    else
       RemoteAddress.sin_addr.S_addr := Inet_Addr(StrPCopy(HostBuf,
FProxy));

    if RemoteAddress.sin_addr.S_addr = SOCKET_ERROR then   //Not already in
IP format
     begin
      RemoteAddress.sin_addr.S_addr := 0;

      wsaasyncgethostbyname(FSocketHandle, WM_WAITFORRESPONSE, HostBuf,
PChar(RemoteHost), MAXGETHOSTSTRUCT);
```

```
   Timedout := false;

   Succeed := false;
   ResolveError := false;
   ThreadTimer.Enabled := true;
   repeat
     Application.ProcessMessages;

   until ResolveError or TimedOut or Canceled or Succeed;

   ThreadTimer.Enabled := false;

   //Handle errors

   if TimedOut then
    begin
      ThrowError(13);
      exit;
    end;

   if Canceled then
    begin
      ThrowError(14);
      exit;
    end;

   if ResolveError then
    begin
      ThrowError(15);
      exit;
    end;

   with RemoteAddress.sin_addr.S_un_b do
     begin
       s_b1 := RemoteHost.h_addr_list^[0];
       s_b2 := RemoteHost.h_addr_list^[1];
       s_b3 := RemoteHost.h_addr_list^[2];
       s_b4 := RemoteHost.h_addr_list^[3];
     end;


   if assigned(FOnHostResolved) then
     FOnHostResolved(self);
end;



if RemoteAddress.sin_addr.S_addr = 0 then
 begin
   ThrowError(15);
   exit;
 end;

RemoteAddress.sin_family := AF_INET; {Make connected true}
```

```
{$R-}
  if FProxy = '' then
    RemoteAddress.sin_port := htons(FPort) {If no proxy get port from Port
property}
  else
    RemoteAddress.sin_port := htons(FProxyPort); {else get port from
ProxyPort property}
{$R+}

  Succeed := false;
  Timedout := false;
  ConnectError := false;



  i := Winsock.Connect(ThisSocket, RemoteAddress, SizeOf(RemoteAddress));
  if (i = INVALID_SOCKET) then
   begin
    if (WSAGetLastError <> WSAEWOULDBLOCK) then
     begin
      ThrowError(18);
      exit; //Check this
     end;
   end;

  ThreadTimer.Enabled := true;
  repeat
    Application.ProcessMessages;

  until (Connected or Canceled or ConnectError or Timedout or Succeed);


  if (Timedout) then
   begin
    RequestCloseSocket;
    ThrowError(19);
    exit;
   end;
  if (Canceled) then
   begin
    RequestCloseSocket;
    ThrowError(14);
    exit;
   end;
  if (ConnectError) then
   begin
    RequestCloseSocket;
    ThrowError(20);
    exit;
   end;
end; //-----------------------------------------------------------------
------

procedure TSSLClientSocket.TimerFired(Sender: TObject);
begin
```

```
   Timedout := true;
   ThreadTimer.Enabled := false;
end;

procedure TSSLClientSocket.RequestCloseSocket;
var
nRet: integer;
szBuf: array[0..255] of char;
begin

  Connected := False;
  if ThisSocket <> TSocket(INVALID_SOCKET) then
    begin
      {Close it}
      shutdown(ThisSocket, 1); //Tell remote server we're not going to
send
      while (true) do
       begin
         nRet := recv(ThisSocket, szBuf, sizeof(szBuf), 0);
         if ((nRet = 0) or (nRet = SOCKET_ERROR)) then
           break;
        end;
      shutdown(ThisSocket, 2); //Tell remote we're not receiving!
      CloseSocket(ThisSocket);

      if not DestroySocket then
        begin
          ThisSocket := Socket(PF_INET, SOCK_STREAM, IPPROTO_IP);
          WSAAsyncselect(ThisSocket, FSocketHandle,
WM_ASYNCHRONOUSPROCESS, FD_OOB or FD_ACCEPT or FD_CONNECT or FD_CLOSE or
FD_READ);
          ThreadTimer.Enabled := false;
        end;

    end;

end; //------------------------------------------------------------------
------

function TSSLClientSocket.ReadBuf(var Buf: array of char; sizebuf:
integer): integer;
var
sz: integer;
aBuf: array[0..MAX_RECV_BUF] of char;
begin
     ZeroMemory(@aBuf, MAX_RECV_BUF+1);
     sz := SSL_read(servercon, aBuf, sizebuf);
     strcopy(Buf, aBuf);
     result := sz;
end;

function TSSLClientSocket.Read: String;
var
sz: integer;
aBuf: array[0..MAX_RECV_BUF] of char;
S: String;
begin
```

```
    ZeroMemory(@aBuf, MAX_RECV_BUF+1);
    sz := SSL_read(servercon, aBuf, 2048);
    S := aBuf;
    result := S;

end;

function TSSLClientSocket.WriteBuf(Buf: array of char; sizebuf: integer):
integer;
var
sz: integer;
begin
    sz := SSL_write(servercon, Buf, sizebuf);
    result := sz;

end;

function TSSLClientSocket.Write(Buf: String; sizebuf: integer): integer;
var
sz: integer;
i: integer;
mBuf: PChar;
sBuf: array[0..MAX_RECV_BUF] of char;

begin
    ZeroMemory(@sBuf, MAX_RECV_BUF+1);
    for i:=0 to Length(Buf)-1 do
     begin
       sBuf[i] := Buf[i+1];
      end;
    //mBuf := StrAlloc(Length(Buf)+1);
    //strcopy(mBuf, PChar(Buf));
    //sz := SSL_write(servercon, mBuf^, sizebuf);
    sz := SSL_write(servercon, sBuf, sizebuf);
    result := sz;

end;

procedure TSSLClientSocket.ClearInput;
var
  Buf: array[0..MAX_RECV_BUF] of Char;
begin
    SSL_read(servercon, Buf, MAX_RECV_BUF)

end; //-----------------------------------------------------------------
------

function TSSLClientSocket.GetRemoteIP: string;
begin
  Result := inet_ntoa(RemoteAddress.sin_addr);
end; //-----------------------------------------------------------------
------

procedure TSSLClientSocket.Disconnect;
begin
```

```
      RequestCloseSocket;

end;


function TSSLClientSocket.GetLocalIP: string;
var
  SockAddrIn: TSockAddrIn;
  Size: Integer;
begin
  Result := '';
  if ThisSocket = INVALID_SOCKET then
    ThrowError(22);

  Size := SizeOf(SockAddrIn);
  try
    if getsockname(thisSocket, SockAddrIn, Size) = 0 then
      Result := inet_ntoa(SockAddrIn.sin_addr);
  except
  end;
end; //-----------------------------------------------------------------
------


////////////////////////////////////////////////////////////////////////
// The Socket Window Definition
////////////////////////////////////////////////////////////////////////
function SSLClientSocketWindowProc(
      ahWnd: HWND;
      auMsg: Integer;
      awParam: WPARAM;
      alParam: LPARAM): Integer; stdcall;
var
   Obj   : TSSLClientSocket;
   MsgRec: TMessage;
begin
   Obj := TSSLClientSocket(GetWindowLong(ahWnd, 0));
   if (( Not Assigned( Obj ))  Or
      ( auMsg < WM_ASYNCHRONOUSPROCESS )) {Or
      //( auMsg > CM_READMESS ))} then // *RAR*
      Result := DefWindowProc(ahWnd, auMsg, awParam, alParam)
   else {_ NOT if not assigned(Obj) then _}
   begin
      MsgRec.Msg := auMsg;
      MsgRec.WPARAM := awParam;
      MsgRec.LPARAM := alParam;
      MsgRec.Result := 0;
//      if (auMsg > WM_USER + 100) and (auMsg < WM_USER + 105) then
      Obj.WndProc(MsgRec);
      Result := MsgRec.Result;
   end; {_ NOT if not assigned(Obj) then _}

end; {_ function PsockWindowProc( _}


var
```

```
    SSLClientSocketWindowClass: TWndClass = (
        Style         : 0;
        lpfnWndproc   : @SSLClientSocketWindowProc;
        cbClsExtra    : 0;
        cbWndExtra    : SizeOf(Pointer);
        HInstance     : 0;
        HICON         : 0;
        HCURSOR       : 0;
        hbrBackground: 0;
        lpszMenuName : nil;
        lpszClassName: 'SSLClientSocketWindowClass');


function SSLClientSocketAllocateHWnd(Obj: TObject): HWND;
var
    TempClass        : TWndClass;
    ClassRegistered: Boolean;
begin
    { Check if the window class is  registered}
    if SSLClientSocketWindowClass.HInstance = 0 then
SSLClientSocketWindowClass.HInstance := HInstance;
    ClassRegistered := GetClassInfo(HInstance,
        SSLClientSocketWindowClass.lpszClassName,
        TempClass);
    if not ClassRegistered then
    begin
        Result := WinProcs.RegisterClass(SSLClientSocketWindowClass);
        if Result = 0 then Exit;
    end; {_ if not ClassRegistered then _}

    { Create a new window                                        }
    Result := CreateWindowEx(WS_EX_TOOLWINDOW,
        SSLClientSocketWindowClass.lpszClassName,
        '', { Window name    }
        WS_POPUP, { Window Style  }
        0, 0, { X, Y             }
        0, 0, { Width, Height }
        0, { hWndParent      }
        0, { hMenu           }
        HInstance, { hInstance      }
        nil); { CreateParam   }


    if (Result <> 0) and assigned(Obj) then
        SetWindowLong(Result, 0, Integer(Obj));

end; {_ function PsockAllocateHWnd(Obj: TObject): HWND; _}




end.
```

OpenSSL and Visual Studio .Net

```
// MyTestLibrary.h
//
// Note had to modify the linker warning:
//Linker Tools Warning LNK4243
//     'DLL containing objects compiled with /clr is not linked with
/NOENTRY; image may not run correctly'.
//
// 1) Link with /NOENTRY. In Solution Explorer, right-click the project
node, click Properties. In the Property Pages dialog box, click Linker,
click Command Line, and then add this switch to the Additional Options
field.
// 2) Link msvcrt.lib. In the Property Pages dialog box, click Linker,
click Input., and then add msvcrt.lib to the Additional Dependencies
property.
// 3) Remove nochkclr.obj. On the Input page (same page as in the previous
step), remove nochkclr.obj from the Additional Dependencies property.
// 4) Link in the CRT. On the Input page (same page as in the previous
step), add __DllMainCRTStartup@12 to the Force Symbol References property.
//
//
// 5-26-04 Modified WM_ASYNCHRONOUSPROCESS, Using WSAGETSELECTEVENT and
WSAGETSELECTERROR rather than directly accessin LParamLo etc, flaky here.
// 5-27-04 Removed OpenSSL_add_all_algorithms. OpenSSL 0.9.7d, no longer
exports this method. Called automatically.
//
#pragma once
#using "mscorlib.dll"
#include "winsock2.h"
#include "windows.h"
#using <System.DLL>
#using <System.Windows.Forms.DLL>




#define WM_ASYNCHRONOUSPROCESS WM_USER+101
#define WM_WAITFORRESPONSE WM_USER+102

#define X509_V_OK                0
#define X509_FILETYPE_PEM            1
#define X509_FILETYPE_ASN1           2
#define X509_FILETYPE_DEFAULT 3
#define NID_commonName           13

#define    SSL_FILETYPE_ASN1    X509_FILETYPE_ASN1
#define    SSL_FILETYPE_PEM     X509_FILETYPE_PEM

#define    RSA_3               0x03
#define    RSA_F4              0x10001

// use either SSL_VERIFY_NONE or SSL_VERIFY_PEER, the last 2 options
```

```
// are 'ored' with SSL_VERIFY_PEER if they are desired
#define     SSL_VERIFY_NONE                 0x00
#define     SSL_VERIFY_PEER                 0x01
#define     SSL_VERIFY_FAIL_IF_NO_PEER_CERT    0x02
#define     SSL_VERIFY_CLIENT_ONCE                 0x04

#define     CRYPTO_NUM_LOCKS     24

#define     CRYPTO_LOCK          1
#define     CRYPTO_UNLOCK                2
#define     CRYPTO_READ          4
#define     CRYPTO_WRITE         8

#define     SSL_SENT_SHUTDOWN               1
#define     SSL_RECEIVED_SHUTDOWN           2
#define     SSL_CTRL_OPTIONS                32
#define     BIO_C_SET_CONNECT               100
#define     BIO_C_GET_FD                    105
#define     BIO_C_SET_NBIO                  102
#define     BIO_C_SET_SSL                           109
#define     BIO_CLOSE                               0x01
#define     BIO_NOCLOSE                     0x00


#define MAX_SOCKET_CONNECTIONS              65000



//SSL TypeDefs for imported functions
//typedef int (*CRYPTO_SET_MEM_FUNCTIONS)(void *(*m)(size_t), void
*(*r)(void *, size_t), void (*f)(void *));
//typedef void (*CRYPTO_SET_LOCKING_CALLBACK)(void (*func)(int Amode,int
Atype, char *Afile,int Aline));
//typedef int (*SSL_LIBRARY_INIT)(void);
//typedef void (*SSL_LOAD_ERROR_STRINGS)(void);
//typedef void *(*SSLV3_CLIENT_METHOD)(void);
//typedef void *(*TLSV1_CLIENT_METHOD)(void);
//typedef void *(*SSLV23_CLIENT_METHOD)(void);
//typedef void *(*OPENSSL_ADD_ALL_ALGORITHMS)(void);
//typedef int (*RAND_LOAD_FILE)(const char *,long);
//typedef void *(*SSL_CTX_NEW)(void *);
//typedef int (*SSL_CTX_SET_CIPHER_LIST)(void *, char *);
//typedef int (*SSL_CTX_USE_CERTIFICATE_FILE)(void *, char *, int);
//typedef int (*SSL_CTX_USE_PRIVATEKEY_FILE)(void *ctx, char *, int);
//typedef int (*SSL_CTX_CHECK_PRIVATE_KEY)(void *ctx);
//typedef void (*ERR_LOAD_CRYPTO_STRINGS)(void);
//typedef int (*SSL_CTX_SET_DEFAULT_VERIFY_PATHS)(void *);
//typedef int (*SSL_CTX_LOAD_VERIFY_LOCATIONS)(void *, char *, char *);
//typedef void *(*BIO_NEW)(void *);
//typedef void *(*BIO_S_CONNECT)(void);
//typedef long (*BIO_CTRL)(void *, int, long, void *);
//typedef void *(*SSL_NEW)(void *);
//typedef void (*SSL_SET_CONNECT_STATE)(void *);
//typedef void (*SSL_SET_BIO)(void *, void *, void *);
//typedef int (*SSL_SET_FD)(void *, SOCKET);
//typedef int (*SSL_CONNECT)(void *);
//typedef int(*SSL_READ)(void *, char *, int);
```

```
//typedef int(*SSL_WRITE)(void *, char *, int);
//typedef int(*SSL_PEEK)(void *, char *, int);
//typedef void (*SSL_FREE)(void *ssl);
//typedef void (*SSL_CTX_SET_DEFAULT_PASSWD_CB)(void *ctx, int
(*passwd_cb)(char &buf, int size, int rwflag, void *userdata));
//typedef void (*SSL_CTX_SET_DEFAULT_PASSWD_CB_USERDATA)(void *ctx, void
*u);
//typedef char *(*ERR_ERROR_STRING)(unsigned long e, char *buf);
//typedef void (*ERR_CLEAR_ERROR)(void);
//typedef unsigned long (*ERR_GET_ERROR)(void);
//typedef void (*SSL_CTX_FREE)(void *ctx);
//typedef int (*SSL_SHUTDOWN)(void *ssl);
//typedef void (*SSL_CTX_FLUSH_SESSIONS)(void *ctx, int tm);

//typedef void (*CRYPTO_SET_LOCKING_CALLBACK)(void (*func));


using namespace System;
using namespace System::Windows::Forms;
using namespace System::Text;
using namespace System::Runtime::InteropServices; //so you can use
DllImport()



namespace MyTestLibrary
{
public __gc class Class1 : public System::Windows::Forms::Control
{
// TODO: Add your methods for this class here.



private:
SOCKET ThisSocket;
bool ConnectError;
bool Succeed;
bool Timedout;

System::Timers::Timer *ConnectTimer;
String* m_Host;
int m_Port;
int m_ConnectMethod;
String* m_KeyPassword;
String* m_LastError;
String* m_CertFile;

String* m_KeyFile;
bool m_UseCertificate;
System::Text::ASCIIEncoding *ase;
HINSTANCE hLib;
HINSTANCE mLib;

bool IPAddress;

protected:
```

```
char* bufHostEnt; //free this when you get a chance!!!
//char bufHostEnt __gc[] = new char __gc[MAXGETHOSTSTRUCT]; //causes
errors here!

public:
//public variables
//__event EventHandler* MyEvent; //testing!!

//SSLeay32 Imports!!
[DllImport("SSLeay32.dll", EntryPoint="SSL_library_init")]
static void SSL_library_init(void);

[DllImport("SSLeay32.dll", EntryPoint="SSL_load_error_strings")]
static void SSL_load_error_strings(void);

[DllImport("SSLeay32.dll", EntryPoint="SSLv3_client_method")]
static void* SSLv3_client_method(void);

[DllImport("SSLeay32.dll", EntryPoint="SSLv2_client_method")]
static void* SSLv2_client_method(void);

[DllImport("SSLeay32.dll", EntryPoint="SSLv23_client_method")]
static void* SSLv23_client_method(void);

[DllImport("SSLeay32.dll", EntryPoint="TLSv1_client_method")]
static void* TLSv1_client_method(void);

[DllImport("SSLeay32.dll", EntryPoint="SSL_CTX_new")]
static void *SSL_CTX_new(void *);

[DllImport("SSLeay32.dll", EntryPoint="SSL_CTX_set_cipher_list")]
static int SSL_CTX_set_cipher_list(void *, char *);

[DllImport("SSLeay32.dll", EntryPoint="SSL_CTX_use_certificate_file")]
static int SSL_CTX_use_certificate_file(void *, char *, int);

[DllImport("SSLeay32.dll", EntryPoint="SSL_CTX_use_PrivateKey_file")]
static int SSL_CTX_use_PrivateKey_file(void *ctx, char *, int);

[DllImport("SSLeay32.dll", EntryPoint="SSL_CTX_check_private_key")]
static int SSL_CTX_check_private_key(void *ctx);

[DllImport("SSLeay32.dll", EntryPoint="SSL_CTX_set_default_verify_paths")]
static int SSL_CTX_set_default_verify_paths(void *);

[DllImport("SSLeay32.dll", EntryPoint="SSL_CTX_load_verify_locations")]
static int SSL_CTX_load_verify_locations(void *, char *, char *);

[DllImport("SSLeay32.dll", EntryPoint="SSL_new")]
static void *SSL_new(void *);

[DllImport("SSLeay32.dll", EntryPoint="SSL_set_connect_state")]
static void SSL_set_connect_state(void *);

[DllImport("SSLeay32.dll", EntryPoint="SSL_set_bio")]
static void SSL_set_bio(void *, void *, void *);
```

```
[DllImport("SSLeay32.dll", EntryPoint="SSL_set_fd")]
static int SSL_set_fd(void *, SOCKET);

[DllImport("SSLeay32.dll", EntryPoint="SSL_connect")]
static int SSL_connect(void *);

[DllImport("SSLeay32.dll", EntryPoint="SSL_read")]
static int SSL_read(void *, char *, int);

[DllImport("SSLeay32.dll", EntryPoint="SSL_write")]
static int SSL_write(void *, char *, int);

[DllImport("SSLeay32.dll", EntryPoint="SSL_peek")]
static int SSL_peek(void *, char *, int);

[DllImport("SSLeay32.dll", EntryPoint="SSL_CTX_set_default_passwd_cb")]
static void SSL_CTX_set_default_passwd_cb(void *ctx, int (*passwd_cb)(char
&buf, int size, int rwflag, void *userdata));

[DllImport("SSLeay32.dll",
EntryPoint="SSL_CTX_set_default_passwd_cb_userdata")]
static void SSL_CTX_set_default_passwd_cb_userdata(void *ctx, void *u);

[DllImport("libeay32.dll", EntryPoint="ERR_error_string")]
static char *ERR_error_string(unsigned long e, char *buf);

[DllImport("libeay32.dll", EntryPoint="ERR_clear_error")]
static void ERR_clear_error(void);

[DllImport("libeay32.dll", EntryPoint="ERR_get_error")]
static unsigned long ERR_get_error(void);

[DllImport("SSLeay32.dll", EntryPoint="SSL_CTX_free")]
static void SSL_CTX_free(void *ctx);

[DllImport("SSLeay32.dll", EntryPoint="SSL_shutdown")]
static int SSL_shutdown(void *ssl);

[DllImport("SSLeay32.dll", EntryPoint="SSL_CTX_flush_sessions")]
static void SSL_CTX_flush_sessions(void *ctx, int tm);

[DllImport("SSLeay32.dll", EntryPoint="SSL_free")]
static void SSL_free(void *ssl);


//libeay32.dll Imports
[DllImport("libeay32.dll", EntryPoint="CRYPTO_set_mem_functions")]
static int CRYPTO_set_mem_functions(void *(*m)(size_t), void *(*r)(void *,
size_t), void (*f)(void *));

[DllImport("libeay32.dll", EntryPoint="CRYPTO_set_locking_callback")]
static void CRYPTO_set_locking_callback(void (*func)(int Amode, int Atype,
char *Afile,int Aline));

[DllImport("libeay32.dll", EntryPoint="RAND_load_file")]
static int RAND_load_file(const char *,long);
```

```
[DllImport("libeay32.dll", EntryPoint="ERR_load_CRYPTO_strings")]
static void ERR_load_CRYPTO_strings(void);

[DllImport("libeay32.dll", EntryPoint="BIO_new")]
static void *BIO_new(void *);

[DllImport("libeay32.dll", EntryPoint="BIO_s_connect")]
static void *BIO_s_connect(void);

[DllImport("libeay32.dll", EntryPoint="BIO_ctrl")]
static long BIO_ctrl(void *, int, long, void *);




bool Connected;
bool Canceled;

void *ssl_ctx;   //BIO Context Underlying SSL
void *meth;      //We are only dealing with meth = SSLv3
void *servercon; //The SSL Connection
bool FSSL;


__event EventHandler* OnRead;
__event EventHandler* OnConnect;
__event EventHandler* OnWrite;
__event EventHandler* OnClose;
__event EventHandler* OnError;

__property String* get_Host()
{
return m_Host;
}

__property void set_Host(String* Value)
{
m_Host = Value;

}

__property int get_Port()
{
return m_Port;
}
__property void set_Port(int Value)
{
m_Port = Value;
}

__property String* get_LastError()
{
return m_LastError;
}
```

```
__property int get_ConnectMethod()
{
return m_ConnectMethod; //0=SSLv2, 1=SSLv23, 2=SSLv3, 3=TLSv1
}

__property void set_ConnectMethod(int Value)
{
m_ConnectMethod = Value; //0=SSLv2, 1=SSLv23, 2=SSLv3, 3=TLSv1
}

__property String* get_KeyPassword()
{
if (m_KeyPassword == 0)
        m_KeyPassword = "";
return m_KeyPassword;
}

__property void set_KeyPassword(String* Value)
{

m_KeyPassword = Value;

}

__property bool get_UseCertificate()
{
return m_UseCertificate;
}

__property void set_UseCertificate(bool Value)
{
m_UseCertificate = Value;
}

__property String* get_CertFile()
{
return m_CertFile;
}

__property void set_CertFile(String* Value)
{
m_CertFile = Value;

}

__property String* get_KeyFile()
{
return m_KeyFile;
}

__property void set_KeyFile(String* Value)
{
m_KeyFile = Value;
}

__property bool get_SSL()
```

```
{
return FSSL;
}

__property void set_SSL(bool Value)
{
FSSL = Value;
}


void Connect()
{

Succeed = false;
Canceled = false;
ConnectError = false;
Connected = false;
Timedout = false;
m_LastError = "";
IPAddress = false;

WSADATA wsaData;
HANDLE hndlTask;



struct in_addr iaDest;
WORD wVersionRequired = MAKEWORD(1,1);
char *ch = NULL;
int nReturnCode;
bufHostEnt = (char *)malloc(MAXGETHOSTSTRUCT);
//Initialize Winsock Environment

nReturnCode = WSAStartup(wVersionRequired, &wsaData);
if (nReturnCode !=0)
        {
                ThrowError(S"Error on WSAStartup.");
                return;

        }
        if (wsaData.wVersion != wVersionRequired)
        {
                ThrowError(S"Wrong Winsock Version");
                return;
        }


        char *myBuf;
        myBuf = (char *)malloc(m_Host->Length+1);
        ZeroMemory(myBuf, m_Host->Length+1);

        for (int i=0;i<=m_Host->Length-1;i++)
        {
                myBuf[i] = m_Host->get_Chars(i);
        }

iaDest.S_un.S_addr = inet_addr(myBuf);
```

```
if (iaDest.S_un.S_addr == INADDR_NONE) //then its a String representation
Address
        {
        hndlTask = WSAAsyncGetHostByName(
                        (HWND)this->Handle.ToInt32(),
                        WM_WAITFORRESPONSE,LPCTSTR(myBuf),
                        bufHostEnt, MAXGETHOSTSTRUCT);
        }
else
        {
        hndlTask = WSAAsyncGetHostByAddr((HWND)this->Handle.ToInt32(),
                WM_WAITFORRESPONSE,
                (char *)&iaDest, sizeof(struct in_addr),
                AF_INET, bufHostEnt, MAXGETHOSTSTRUCT);

        IPAddress = true;

        }
free(myBuf); //free the memory!!
if (hndlTask == 0 && IPAddress == false)
        {
                ThrowError("Error Resolving Host");
                return;
        }
}

if (FSSL) {
        if (!Load_SSL_Library())
        {
                ThrowError("Could not load SSL library");
                return;
        }
        }
if (FSSL)
                if (!SetCTX())
                {
                ThrowError("Could not load SSL Context");
                return;
                }


}//end Connect Method, hopefully we went to StartConnection


bool Load_SSL_Library()
{
int i;
SSL_library_init();
SSL_library_init();
SSL_load_error_strings();
return true;

}//--------------------------------------------------------------------
------------


bool SetCTX()
```

```
{
char ch[3000];
int ret;
int i;

unsigned long e;
char errorbuf[255];
bool errorout;

int width;
void *conn; //use to be Pointer
bool useSSL;

int nRet;


for (i=0;i<=3000;i++) //could use memset, but on the safe side
        ch[i] = 0x00;

// xSSLeayInit; Already Called in Load_SSL_Library!
if (m_ConnectMethod == 2)
        meth = SSLv3_client_method();
else
        if (m_ConnectMethod == 1)
                meth = SSLv23_client_method();
        else
                if (m_ConnectMethod == 0)
                        meth = SSLv2_client_method();
                else
                        meth = TLSv1_client_method();


//OpenSSL_add_all_algorithms();

nRet = RAND_load_file(".rnd", 0x100000);

ssl_ctx = NULL;
ssl_ctx = SSL_CTX_new(meth);


if (m_KeyPassword != 0)
{
        char pBuf[40];
        memset(pBuf, 0, 40);


        for (int i=0; i<=m_KeyPassword->Length - 1;i++)
        {
                pBuf[i] = m_KeyPassword->get_Chars(i);
        }

        SSL_CTX_set_default_passwd_cb_userdata(ssl_ctx, pBuf);

}
```

175

```
if (m_UseCertificate)
{

        char *FCertFile;
        char *FKeyFile;
        if (m_CertFile != 0)
        {
                FCertFile = (char *)malloc(m_CertFile->Length+1);

                for (int x=0;x<=m_CertFile->Length -1;x++)
                {
                        FCertFile[x] = m_CertFile->get_Chars(x);
                }
                FCertFile[x] = '\0';

                if (SSL_CTX_use_certificate_file(ssl_ctx, FCertFile,
SSL_FILETYPE_PEM) <= 0)
                {
                        free(FCertFile);
                        ThrowError("File does not exist or there was an
error reading the certificate file.");
                        return false;
                }
        }


        if (m_KeyFile != 0)
        {
                FKeyFile = (char *)malloc(m_KeyFile->Length+1);
                for (int x=0;x<=m_KeyFile->Length -1;x++)
                {
                        FKeyFile[x] = m_KeyFile->get_Chars(x);
                }
                FKeyFile[x] = '\0';

                if (SSL_CTX_use_PrivateKey_file(ssl_ctx, FKeyFile,
SSL_FILETYPE_PEM) <= 0)
                {

                        i = ERR_get_error(); //get last error code
                        ERR_error_string(i, errorbuf);

                        ERR_clear_error();
                        ERR_clear_error();
                        ERR_clear_error();

                        //KeyPassword is not accurate or missing
                        if ((i == 151429224) || (i == 101077092))
                        {
                                do {
                                        errorout = true;
```

```
                                swordRequired(this, errorout);

                                char passBuf[40];
                                memset(passBuf, 0, 40);

                                for (int i=0; i<=m_KeyPassword-
>Length - 1;i++)
                                {
                                        passBuf[i] = m_KeyPassword-
>get_Chars(i);
                                }


        SSL_CTX_set_default_passwd_cb_userdata(ssl_ctx, passBuf);

                                if
(SSL_CTX_use_PrivateKey_file(ssl_ctx, FKeyFile, SSL_FILETYPE_PEM) <= 0)
                                {
                                if (errorout)
                                        {
                                                //MUST ERROR OUT
COMPLETELY!
                                                ERR_clear_error();
                                                free(FKeyFile);
                                                ThrowError("There was
an error with the password to the private key file.  Please try again.");
                                                return false;
                                        }
                                        ERR_clear_error();
                                }
                                else
                                        break; //password is ok!!
Whoo Whoo!
                                }
                        while (true);

                }
                else
                {

                        ERR_clear_error();
                        free(FKeyFile);
                        ThrowError("There was an error with the
password to the private key file.  Please try again.");
                        return false;
                }
        }

        free(FKeyFile);
        if (!SSL_CTX_check_private_key(ssl_ctx))
                {
                        ThrowError("There was a general error
checking the private key file.  Error 37");
                        return false;
                }
    }
}
```

```
ERR_load_CRYPTO_strings();
return true;

}
void StartConnection()
{
int nRet = 0;
SOCKADDR_IN saServ;
LPHOSTENT lpHostEntry;
struct in_addr iaDest;




saServ.sin_port = htons(m_Port);
saServ.sin_family = AF_INET;

lpHostEntry = (hostent *)bufHostEnt;

if (IPAddress)
{


        char *myBuf;
        myBuf = (char *)malloc(m_Host->Length+1);
        ZeroMemory(myBuf, m_Host->Length+1);


        for (int i=0;i<=m_Host->Length-1;i++)
        {
                myBuf[i] = m_Host->get_Chars(i);
        }



        saServ.sin_addr.S_un.S_addr = inet_addr(myBuf);
        free(myBuf);
}
else
{
saServ.sin_addr = *((LPIN_ADDR)*lpHostEntry->h_addr_list);
}

ThisSocket = socket(AF_INET, SOCK_STREAM, 0);
if (ThisSocket == SOCKET_ERROR)
{
        ThrowError("Socket Error - Could not create SOCKET");
        return;
}
if (WSAAsyncSelect(ThisSocket, (HWND)this->Handle.ToInt32(),
        WM_ASYNCHRONOUSPROCESS, FD_CONNECT | FD_READ | FD_WRITE |
FD_CLOSE))
{
```

```
        ThrowError("Socket Error - Could not assign AsyncSelect");
        return;
}

nRet = connect(ThisSocket, (LPSOCKADDR)&saServ, sizeof(SOCKADDR_IN));
ConnectError = false;
Succeed = false;
Timedout = false;
if (nRet == SOCKET_ERROR)
{
        if (WSAGetLastError() != WSAEWOULDBLOCK)
        {

                ThrowError("WSAEWOULDBLOCK Error");
                return;
        }

}
free(bufHostEnt); //Can free this resource now
}//end StartConnection!!


void Disconnect()
{

closesocket(ThisSocket);
shutdown(ThisSocket, 0);
Connected = false;
Canceled = true;
if (FSSL)
{
        __try
        {
                SSL_free(servercon);
                SSL_shutdown(servercon);
                free(bufHostEnt);

        }
        __finally
        {
                //nothing!!
        }
}


//Fire On Disconnect!

}



int ReadBuf(unsigned char buf __gc[], int size)
{

int i = 0;
int rc = 0;
char *myBuf;
```

```
myBuf = (char *)malloc(size);
ZeroMemory(myBuf, size);


if (FSSL)
      rc = SSL_read(servercon, myBuf, size);
else
      rc = recv(ThisSocket, myBuf, size, 0);


//There has to be a better method!!
for (i=0; i<=rc-1; i++)
{
      buf[i] = myBuf[i];
}

free(myBuf);
return rc;


}

int SendBuf(unsigned char buf __gc[], int size)
{

int rc = 0;
int i = 0;
char *myBuf;
myBuf = (char *)malloc(size+1);
ZeroMemory(myBuf, size+1);

//There has to be a better method!
for (i=0; i<=size-1; i++)
{
      myBuf[i] = buf[i];
}

if (FSSL)
      rc = SSL_write(servercon, myBuf, size);
else
      rc = send(ThisSocket, myBuf, size, 0);

return rc;

}

void ThrowError(String* errString)
{

Console::WriteLine(errString);
m_LastError = errString;
OnError(this, new System::EventArgs());


}


protected:
```

```
//The infamous WndProc Method!!!!
void Class1::WndProc(System::Windows::Forms::Message* m)
{
//ThrowError(m->Msg.ToString());
int swInt;
swInt = Convert::ToInt32(m->Msg);



switch (swInt) {


        case WM_WAITFORRESPONSE:

                if (WSAGETASYNCERROR(m->LParam.ToPointer()))
                {
                                if (IPAddress)
                                {
                                        Console::WriteLine("Resolution of IP
not necessary...already in IPv4 form");
                                        StartConnection();
                                }
                                else
                                {
                                        bool ResolveError = true;
                                        ThrowError("Windows could not resolve
host");
                                }
                }
                else
                {
                        //Succeed = true;
                        Console::WriteLine("Socket Resolved");
                        StartConnection();
                }
                //ShowMessage("Got Response");
                break;
        case WM_ASYNCHRONOUSPROCESS:
                int x = m->LParam.ToInt32();
                int y = WSAGETSELECTEVENT(x);
                int z = WSAGETSELECTERROR(x);
                if (WSAGETSELECTERROR(x) > 0)
                        ConnectError = true;
                else
                {

                        Succeed = true;
                        //Console::WriteLine("Connected");
                }

                switch (WSAGETSELECTEVENT(x)) {
                //switch (LOWORD(Convert::ToInt32(m->LParam.ToInt32()))) {

                        case FD_CONNECT:
                                if (Succeed)
                                {
```

```
                                        if (Canceled)
                                                break;
                                        if (FSSL)
                                                SetSSL3();

                                        Connected = true;
                                        //Console::WriteLine("FD_CONNECT");
                                        OnConnect(this, new
System::EventArgs()); //Testing this Event!!



                                }
                                else
                                {
                                        String *S = "Error on connecting ";
                                        S-
>Concat(WSAGetLastError().ToString());

                                        ThrowError(S);
                                }
                                break;
                        case FD_READ:
                                        if (Canceled)
                                                break;
                                        //Console::WriteLine("FD_READ");
                                        //FireReadEvent();
                                        OnRead(this, new
System::EventArgs()); //Testing this Event!!
                                        break;
                        case FD_CLOSE:

                                        //Console::WriteLine("FD_CLOSE");
                                        if (Connected)
                                        {
                                                //ClearInput;
                                                Connected = false;
                                                OnClose(this, new
System::EventArgs()); //Testing this Event!!
                                        }
                                        //FireOnDisconnect();
                                        //RequestCloseSocket();

                                        break;
                        case FD_WRITE:
                                        if (Canceled)
                                                break;
                                        //Console::WriteLine("FD_WRITE");
                                        OnWrite(this, new
System::EventArgs()); //Testing this Event!!
                                        break;
                } //end inner switch


                break; //WM_ASYNCHRONOUSPROCESS
}//end of switch
```

```
Control::WndProc(m); //Call the base class method!
}

bool SetSSL3()
{
char ch[3000];
int ret;
int i;

unsigned long e;
char errorbuf[255];
bool errorout;

int width;
void *conn; //use to be Pointer
bool useSSL;

int nRet;
//  FinSSL = false;


//  ---------THIS IS SERVER AUTHENTICATION; NOT USING -------------------
-----------
//    ret = (*SSL_CTX_set_default_verify_paths)(ssl_ctx);
//    if (ret <= 0)
//    {
//      ret = ret; //debugging
//    }
//    ret = SSL_CTX_load_verify_locations(ssl_ctx, NULL, NULL);
//    if (ret <= 0)
//    {
//      ret = ret; //Need CA trusted?
//    }
//  -------------------------------------------------------------------

            conn = NULL;  //just checking...
            conn = BIO_new(BIO_s_connect());
            if (conn == NULL)
            {
                    //ThrowError(38,"",true);
                    return false;
            }
            //Make the underlying BIO a non-blocking socket!
            ret = BIO_ctrl(conn,BIO_C_SET_NBIO,1,NULL);
            if (ret <= 0)
            {

                    return false;
            }

                    servercon = NULL; //just checking...
                    servercon = SSL_new(ssl_ctx);
                    SSL_set_connect_state(servercon);
                    SSL_set_bio(servercon, conn, conn);
```

```
width = SSL_set_fd(servercon, ThisSocket) + 1;

do {

        i = SSL_connect(servercon);

        if (Canceled)
                break; //out of do loop!
} while (!((i > 0)));

if (Canceled)
{
        Disconnect();
        ThrowError("SSL Connection Canceled");

        return false;
}


if ((!Connected) && (i <= 0))
        {
                ThrowError("Connection was closed.  Please
try again.");
                return false;
        }
else
        if (i <= 0)
        {
                Disconnect();
                ThrowError("Could not connect in SSL.
Return value from SSL less than 0.");
                return false;
        }


    return true;

}//-----------------------------------------------------------------------
```

Summary

OpenSSL is a great implementation and as far as an open source product goes, offers a great toolkit! This document is intended for use with the Visual SSL product from Trizen Systems which offers custom SSL components utilizing the OpenSSL libraries for Delphi and Borland C++ Builder. It was our intent **not** to show the theory behind SSL, because as anyone can tell you there is a lot of theory on the subject, but rather to demonstrate how SSL is actually used within Windows. If you would like to get more information please visit http://www.openssl.org for a good bit of information as well as looking in the C:\OpenSSL\openssl-0.9.6a\docs directory for information on commands and applications.

It goes without saying, but by only experimenting with SSL can you really learn about what the product can accomplish. We highly suggest you play with the switches for the *s_client* and *s_server* applications.

We hope you will carry the torch for the OpenSSL project and implement SSL into all of your applications. For implementation examples you can purchase the Visual SSL source code and/or the Visual 3270 source code for your review.

Index